C000196083

Three Generations of
RAILWAYMEN

THREE GENERATIONS OF
RAILWAYMEN

JIM, GEOFF AND IAN BODY

First published 2018

The History Press
The Mill, Brimscombe Port
Stroud, Gloucestershire, GL5 2QG
www.thehistorypress.co.uk

© Geoff Body, Ian Body, 2018

The right of Geoff Body and Ian Body to be identified as
the Authors of this work has been asserted in accordance with the
Copyright, Designs and Patents Act 1988.

All rights reserved. No part of this book may be reprinted
or reproduced or utilised in any form or by any electronic,
mechanical or other means, now known or hereafter invented,
including photocopying and recording, or in any information
storage or retrieval system, without the permission in writing
from the Publishers.

British Library Cataloguing in Publication Data.
A catalogue record for this book is available from the British Library.

ISBN 978 0 7509 8806 3

Typesetting and origination by The History Press
Printed and bound by CPI Group (UK) Ltd

CONTENTS

PART THREE: IAN BODY

INTRODUCTION AND ACKNOWLEDGEMENTS

When Jim Body joined the Great Northern Railway in June 1916, just after his 13th birthday, the rail network was at its peak, with nearly 24,000 miles of its rails covering the whole country and pervading every aspect of life. Now it has shrunk to less than half its former size and is a totally different activity, one that he would barely have recognised. In the way of these things, there is now a move to reverse something of the long, lean years of line closures which, in doctrinal haste, cost so many important transport routes, such as the Great Central route to Marylebone, and various cross-country lines including those from the Midlands to King's Lynn and from Oxford to Cambridge.

Jim was born in rural Lincolnshire into a family with a long history as agricultural labourers. His schooling progress provided an opportunity for a major change, and engagement as a lad trainee on the railway, then a highly regarded employment, was a major change in his life. How strange his first days must have been, with the journey to the gaunt railway district office at Peterborough, an interview with austere officials and then arriving at his first station. There he would have been plunged into a world of myriad forms and practices, as well as the earthy excitement of being part of the train romance that he had only known of vaguely before.

The amount of railway change in Jim's lifetime was incredible, not just in the trains, track and signalling but also in functional matters – all, of course, in stages which Jim needed to understand and embrace. He would have seen two world wars, with the 1923 grouping and the contrast of the General Strike and the dawn of the glamour expresses in between. He was dedicated and loyal to the railway industry and its tradition of public service, and maintained his belief in its traditions for the whole of his fifty-two years of service. This dedication and his ability took the lad trainee to a final well-deserved senior post as a divisional traffic accountant.

Unsurprisingly, Jim communicated much of his enthusiasm for railways to his son, Geoff, who joined the old London & North Eastern Railway at the age of 16 in 1945. The whole system had emerged from the demands of a second major war, worn out but hopeful. It still operated in much the same way but had high hopes for the future which the LNER expressed in a modernisation plan labelled 'Forward'. In his progression from temporary probationary junior male clerk to senior officer, Geoff was also to be part of great changes in Britain's railways. The Modernisation Plan of 1954 brought vehicles like railbuses and diesel locomotives; suburban electrification followed and then the overhead lines linked Euston and Glasgow. Semaphore signals and level crossings were modernised, speeds rose dramatically and every facet of the activity improved. But road competition was not to be denied, earnings dropped and Dr Beeching's 'reshaping' plan led to a climate of closure which was eventually to see not only a huge reduction in the route mileage but also, in due course, the abandonment of the traditional wagon-load business, newspaper and postal traffic, and the Red Star Parcels service. Privatisation completed the massive changes.

After twenty-eight years, Geoff moved on to managing a road tanker company and subsequently to his own writing and publishing activities which, unsurprisingly, had railways at their core.

By the time Ian joined the railway, this general process of change was continuing, albeit mostly in a downward trend with the early 1980s representing the lowest point for revenue and growth. In 1986, sectorisation saw the arrival of the three passenger subdivisions of InterCity, Regional Railways and Network South East, and things generally began to pick up. The arrival of high-speed trains (HSTs) exemplified the optimism and rate of change along with serious restructuring of the freight business. This process of change was further accelerated by the Railways Act of 1993 which heralded privatisation. While the company names and liveries were perhaps the most obvious change to the public eye, the separation of infrastructure and rolling stock ownership from operation were far more fundamental. Passenger carryings continued to rise significantly, the railways opened their doors to much more external recruitment and the industry began to be judged against other industries rather than as a traditional category of its own. In some ways it had come full circle from Jim's days in terms of private ownership, coupled with dramatically advanced operation and technical expertise, but comfortingly, the underlying values of public service and industry comradeship had not changed.

The direct and indirect railway links of these three lives span over a century. In that time they have brought the three people involved great dividends from those they have worked with and the experiences they have gained. We are grateful for both and for the ongoing support for this record provided by Amy Rigg and her colleagues at The History Press.

All photographs are from the authors' collection except where specifically acknowledged.

PART ONE

HERBERT (JIM) BODY

By Geoff Body

LAD TRAINEE TO STATION RELIEF CLERK 🐦

My father was Herbert Body, 'Young Jim' as everyone called him at first, and then just 'Jim'. He was born into an agricultural worker's family at Heckington in Lincolnshire in 1903 but grew up at Great Ponton when they moved there in that same year. Such moves were commonplace in the farming world at that time and the next one was to Corby, only 5 miles away but providing advancement for young Jim's father, who was given control of the farm's steam machinery. Curiously, a son of the family living next door turned out to be C.K. Bird, who ultimately rose to the top ranks of the London & North Eastern Railway (LNER).

A Lowly Start

Father himself was destined for a railway career, showing enough educational promise to raise the prospect of a scholarship to Grantham Grammar School. Then fate took a hand, as is so often the case, and an opening occurred for a lad trainee on the Great Northern Railway (GNR) at Great Ponton station, on the King's Cross to York main line. Backed by his headmaster, young Jim secured an interview at the GNR District Office at Peterborough, was appointed to the position at Great Ponton and began his railway career there on 19 June 1916. By now the family had again moved home and the novice railwayman had to find lodgings. This he did, but at 13 his wage was a mere

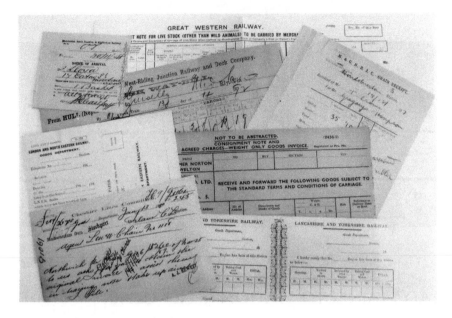

Examples of the multitude of forms young Jim Body would have had to understand and use when he began his railway career at Great Ponton station.

9s a week, which was less than he had to pay out for his accommodation. Not for the last time, a parental subsidy was needed.

Life at Great Ponton station would hardly have been hectic. It lay on the 5 miles of 1 in 200 descent northwards from Stoke Tunnel, where Down trains would have been braking for Grantham and Up ones steaming hard to breast the crest and speed down the high-speed stretch beyond the tunnel. The local passenger train service was sparse because of the line occupation demands of the long-distance expresses, and the trains that did call would break no speed records. The first Down train to call was part way through its all-stations marathon from King's Cross to Doncaster, which occupied nearly seven hours in the process. When he was qualified, Dad would have booked a handful of people going to work on the 8.32 a.m. and then watched as the guard waved his green flag and the locomotive, probably an Ivatt 4-4-0, eased its train off towards Grantham and the connections it made there for the Nottingham, Lincoln and Boston lines. He may well have lingered to watch an Ivatt Atlantic storming the gradient on the Up line and marvelled at the graceful 4-4-2 locomotive, a design which had appeared on the main-line scene in 1902 and was to be the mainstay of its express services for nearly fifty years. Off he would then go to tackle the daily cash balance, some goods traffic invoicing and other routine station tasks.

A Move, a War and a Scare

Things were a bit more lively at Waddington, where Dad was sent after his five-month induction at Great Ponton. The passenger train service on the line running north from Grantham to Lincoln in the shadow of the Wold ridge was a little busier, especially on Lincoln fair or market days, but the station's main activity was linked to the new aerodrome situated some 5 miles to the east beyond Waddington village.

The Great War began to rage fiercely and air power was becoming increasingly important, and with it the needs of the new aerodrome up on the hill. Its personnel, supplies and construction materials all had to come by rail and the modest Up side goods yard at the station was a busy place indeed. The constant stream of inwards rail traffic all had to be hand-craned onto flat trailers and then hauled up the steep hill by a traction engine. Between issuing tickets and keeping the goods office records, Dad found himself with plenty to keep him occupied.

Now 13½, Dad had got a rise with the move. His rate was now 12s 6d for a week of ten-hour days. Unfortunately, his 'digs' cost half a crown more, so the parental subsidy had to continue to make up the deficit and help with clothing, books and the like. He fell for the sister of a new-found friend, a farmer's daughter who lived just across the road from the station and who was destined to become my mother, but there was no cash to spare for romantic gestures at this period.

No doubt there were occasional lively moments, one at least proving quite unusual and not a little scary. It was a time when German Zeppelins were already raiding the east of England and, looking up on one occasion, Dad knew that the dark shape overhead boded no good. It proved to be a Zeppelin which had followed the course of the railway line, looking for targets to bomb. All this passed quickly through young Jim's mind and his worst fears seemed to be realised when a dark object was lobbed out of the passing airship and hurtled down towards him. Jim had never run faster in his young life until a resounding clang on the station approach road revealed the object to be an empty fuel can!

A Very Different Scene

In 1921, now 18, Jim became a man clerk and got a nice rise to £80 a year. With the wartime activity at Waddington now at an end, he was moved to an office at Stainby. There a new aspect of the railway business confronted him on a mineral line network which ran west from the main line at High Dyke to serve a growing activity in the mining of iron ore. Opened in 1920 to serve mines either side of the route at Colsterworth, the single line continued on to more mines and sidings at Stainby and was then extended to Sproxton in 1923. Working the branch was a pretty basic operation, with unusual and often slightly hair-raising operating practices and the need to manage and document a large number of empty wagons coming in and constant loads of ore hauled outwards over steep gradients and sharp curves to the main-line marshalling sidings at High Dyke.

Jim again had to lodge, this time at Colsterworth and with a signalman who worked the Stainby signal box, one Harry Barlow whom he described as 'quite a card'. With station working and the mineral line business all adding to his experience, after a couple of years Jim got a nice promotion to be a station relief clerk based at Hitchin. Another change brought him back to be based in district manager 'Micky' Mirfield's office at Peterborough, again relieving holidays and vacancies anywhere between 'Arlesey and Arksey' as he was wont to describe it. It was a varied and interesting job, with the occasional drama. One attended his period relieving at Rossington, where the passengers were mainly coal miners. Dad was a small, compact man, dwarfed by the burly miners, but he still had to deal with those who showed a marked reluctance to pay for their travel and others who returned from Doncaster races after having drowned the sorrows of their betting losses.

Married

With much improved financial prospects and a colleague offering him a terraced house to rent for 4s a week, Jim and his Waddington sweetheart could now marry. This they did back at Waddington in 1927, and two years later they produced a son who was to be the family's second-generation railwayman. My mother returned to the family home to await my arrival and stayed there for eight weeks before bringing the young lad back with her to Peterborough. Dad, ever meticulous, kept a housekeeping record during that period, faithfully recording everything from his wages of £2 7s 6d a week to such things as bread 4d and the shilling for his

FIG. 97.—Stirling's Famous " Eight-footer." (*Photo, G.N.R.*)

FIG. 98.—The Last Word in Locomotives : Great Northern " Pacific."
(*Photo, G.N.R.*)

Great Northern Railway locomotives Jim Body would have seen at work.

membership of the Railway Clerks' Association. The week of my return was marked with her train fare of 9s 6d, a 3s taxi fare and 1s 9d for 'gripe water'. A new era had begun.

THE SECOND WORLD WAR 🏴

System Streamlining

The war years of 1939 to 1945 were to place a huge strain on the railway system, producing a large increase in traffic but with manpower ranks depleted by the needs of the armed forces. One measure that had to be taken was to eliminate all waste and inefficiency, and to this end a task force was set up and six posts were advertised to secure experienced staff to scrutinise activity at all main centres throughout the Southern Area of the LNER, to streamline practices there and to reduce staffing requirements accordingly. My father saw this vacancy list, with the result that 'For some reason now obscure I applied for a post in London,' to quote from the memoirs I later bludgeoned him into writing. He was successful in securing one of the positions and was to spend several years contributing to the war effort in this way. It was not always popular, of course, leading to the people concerned being known as 'The Razor Gang'. His base was Marylebone but, because of the London bombing, he was allowed to continue living in Peterborough, where my mother did her bit by becoming an unpaid cashier at the city's American Red Cross club.

Dad managed to get home most weekends but then had reports to write and Home Guard and fire-watching duties to carry out. By this time the Home Guard had graduated from its origins as the Local Defence Volunteers (known colloquially as the Look, Duck and Vanish brigade) into being properly armed with rifles. Even so, he regarded a period of duty on the roof of Peterborough North station as a bit risky at a time when the main danger came from the air.

Like countless others, our family, now with a daughter, had to cope with food rationing, air raids spent in the Morrison shelter and other difficulties, but Dad never faltered. Always smart, from gold tie pin to spats, he scoured the LNER lost property office in the motley King's Cross buildings, known by most as 'The African Jungle', for items which would help with the wartime shortages. He could never resist a bargain umbrella but did better at nearby Bravingtons, where the 10 per cent discount afforded to REPTA (Railway Employees Privilege Ticket Association) members went towards a tasteful piece of jewellery for his wife.

Dead of Night

By 1943, the theft and pilferage taking place on the railways to feed the black market had reached serious proportions and a headquarters decision was taken to appoint a team of two experienced people to track down where the losses were occurring and devise ways of combating them. Dad was chosen to represent the railway operating and commercial role in this process, and Inspector Bill Baker of Grimsby that of the railway police. Together they began an intense period of visiting depots, docks and yards, working with local staff and police officers, spending uncomfortable hours in goods yards and depots watching for criminal activity and enduring the horrors of the Luftwaffe's attempts to bomb the railways into dysfunction. Dad rarely alluded to the horrors of the bombing nights, just joking about his appreciation of the solid LNER tables he often had to shelter under. But he was, not unreasonably, proud of the results achieved in arrests and prosecutions, sadly mostly of railway employees, and in the reduction in losses and claims. After a nearby clothing factory had been bombed while Dad was keeping an eye on the wagons loaded with Player's cigarettes in Nottingham goods yard, he was greatly upset for many years by the cries of the injured he had heard.

Dad enjoyed having first-class travel for the first time in this period, but overnight observation from an unheated guard's van or crouching in an empty platelayers' hut while incendiary bombs dropped nearby was considerably less of a pleasure. Twice having to convince others that he was not a German spy also came in the latter category.

TO NORFOLK POST-WAR ▶

Weary of the war, as everyone was, but with an official letter of recognition of his work, Dad returned to his pre-war post at Peterborough. Promotion from Class III to Class II came in 1946 with a successful application for a staff inspecting clerk position in the Norwich district office, and the family duly moved to that fine city. Dad was to spend twenty-two happy years in Norwich, twenty of them based in the railway offices housed in the impressive main building at Thorpe station.

By this time I, too, was a railwayman and was now working at stations in the Norwich district. I don't think there was any nepotism but Dad had a good relationship with the chief staff clerk, Cyril Birkett, which may have helped in the variety of postings that enhanced my learning process. By the time I came back after a period elsewhere, Dad was head of the General Section and subsequently joined the management staff level as assistant to the district manager.

The End of the M&GN

In 1959, Dad had to take on a task for which his Razor Gang work had well qualified him. It was the time of closures and the wandering routes of the old Midland & Great Northern (M&GN) railway network in north Norfolk were never going to survive. Busy as its main line from

On 2 January 1959 the 11.37 a.m. from Cromer Beach calls at Holt on its way to Norwich City. Just two months later most of the M&GN system will lose all its passenger services.

Castle Bytham to Great Yarmouth may have been on summer Saturdays, a weekday journey labouring over its 150 miles of mixed single- and double-line route just did not earn enough to service its costs. The other main M&GN routes from King's Lynn to Peterborough and Melton Constable to Norwich had to go too.

Despite the magnitude of the closure task, it was achieved – sadly in some ways. But this was still the period when redundant railway items were sold off cheaply to staff and the family acquired one or two mementoes of a route they had some affection for, including an Eastern & Midlands Railway platform seat, now in the care of a preservation location. The standard cost, whatever the item, was 5s, and proof of ownership was recognised by the issue of a 'Firewood Receipt' by the district engineer's office.

Relays and Punched Cards

My father's last post was that of divisional accountant at Norwich, a position from which he retired on 20 April 1968 after just two months less then fifty-two years of varied and useful railway service.

Jim Body seated at his desk as the Norwich Division traffic accountant.

Quite apart from the natural affection of son for father, I had a special regard for a man who could successfully make the journey from the laborious clerical and accounting routines of his first years to managing the new generation of huge IBM relay computers and punched card accounting. In between he had seen the full variety of his industry in many places and guises, and he never lost his affection for it and his pride in it.

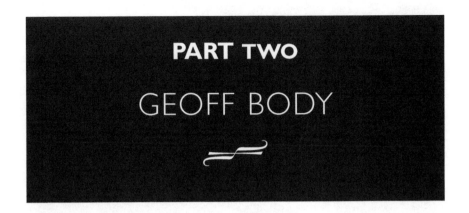

PART TWO

GEOFF BODY

UNDER THE INFLUENCE

Records Smashed

It was supposed to be a secret but I have no doubt that the railway grapevine had been at work and that quite a few people knew about it. Not me, though. At just 6 years old I could hardly have been aware of the excitement that had been steadily growing on the London & North Eastern Railway, spreading through Doncaster Works and the Marylebone headquarters and then seeping out to other parts of the LNER empire. All I knew was that my dad had promised me an exciting outing.

It was September 1935, four months after the Silver Jubilee celebrations of King George V and Queen Mary. On the 27th, a Friday, I was up, washed and dressed far too early, and eager to set out with my father, then an LNER relief clerk working at whatever stations in the Peterborough district needed temporary assistance. After what seemed an impossible wait, we eventually left the house, caught the Eastern Counties company's red double-decker bus to Peterborough North station and crossed to the Down side of what was still known as the Great Northern main line, before settling down to wait.

Still with no idea what it was all about, I do remember a stir among the small crowd, people fidgeting, looking at their watches and waiting for movement among the approach signals. And then it happened. Passing within a few yards of me was a train such as I had never seen in any of the rail journeys we had made to visit other members of the family – a sleek

Streamlined A4 Pacific No 2509 *Silver Link* at Hadley Wood with the 1935 inaugural LNER Silver Jubilee train. The sight of this later in its journey inspired in Geoff Body his choice of a railway career.

silver-grey locomotive and matching coaches, so unlike the regular LNER, LMS (London, Midland & Scottish) and M&GN visitors to Peterborough.

Class A4 Pacific No 2509 *Silver Link* and its train had reduced speed to negotiate the curves that then existed in the Peterborough alignment and I had no idea of what had already been achieved. The speed over the 41 miles between Hatfield and Huntingdon had averaged just over 100mph and four world records were to be broken during this short press preview run to Grantham, a fitting commemoration of this, the 110th anniversary of the pioneer Stockton & Darlington Railway and the dawn of a new era.

Lines of Character

Another strong influence on my subsequent choice of career was linked to our family visits to Stamford, where we 'took tea' with an elderly aunt and uncle in a fashion I thought quaint and they clearly thought 'proper'. Despite then accommodating heavy traffic on the Great North Road, Stamford was, and still is, an attractive place, full of character and enhanced by its many warm stone buildings. Our journey was made on a stopping train from Peterborough with a change at Essendine for the short single-line branch to Stamford. The station there, later called Stamford East, was a fine Tudor-style building, reflecting the influence of Burghley House, the home of the Marquis of Exeter, who was a prime mover in the promotion and funding of the branch railway.

Stamford had realised quickly that it needed to take action to compensate for missing out on the newly opened Great Northern main line to the north, which had passed it by to the east. By 1853, the Stamford & Essendine Railway had secured its enabling Act for a branch to the GNR and was opened three years later. As the major shareholder, the marquis had influenced the design of its station headquarters and, for a time, some staff wore a special livery. The decorative frontage of the station building led to a square booking hall with a high ceiling and a gallery around the first-floor level. Huge doors then led to the single covered platform with its two faces and sidings beyond.

Essendine, GNR main-line junction for the Stamford and Bourne branches which provided Geoff Body with both his first footplate experience and his first writing fee.

The whole station, although not huge, was incredibly imposing, and being allowed to ascend the footplate of a branch tank locomotive on our arriving train cemented the indelible impression the place made on me. Later visits, in a position of some authority, never diminished that initial impression, even knowing that the signalmen were able in quiet moments to do a spot of fishing in the River Welland from the top of the signal-box steps. This just added to the delightful idiosyncrasy of the place, as did the fact that soon after the GNR took over the line its 0-4-2 tank locomotive No 503 managed to plunge itself into the same river and acquire the soubriquet 'The Welland Diver' when recovered. Dad also passed on the account of local man Jim Cherry about a bull going berserk in the goods yard, ending up stranded in the river and having to be lassoed in the course of a hectic mini rodeo to get it out again.

Retracing our steps homeward took us past the junction for the closed branch to Wansford, another modest venture serving a sparse territory and an early closure victim. At one period, supposedly, the controlling Stamford station master visited this part of his empire on horseback, and it was certainly unusual in having its train-loading restrictions expressed as maximum wheels per train. Nor was the shadow of the past entirely escaped back at the main-line junction station, for Essendine's other branch was equally eccentric, with its own unusual coaching stock where the train guard was wont to polish the brasswork. An article on that line's closure earned the author his first writing fee, a princely £2.

A Main-Line Junction

Another factor in my eventual choice of career was one more outing with Dad, this time when he was working a shift in the passimeter at Peterborough East. Passimeters were a recent LNER innovation and comprised a ticket office with windows all round, and positioned so that joining passengers were channelled along one side and alighting ones the other. My job was to receive and sort the collected tickets at the latter.

Closed in 1966, East station had, in fact, served the city's original railway line, that from Northampton which had arrived via the valley of the adjacent River Nene in 1845 and then been linked with Ely. The direct Stamford line followed to create an important link between the Midlands and the East Coast. Before its closure and short resurrection as a depot for BRUTEs (British Rail Universal Trolley Equipment), the station had services along the lines to Ely and beyond and west to Northampton, Rugby and Leicester. It was unusual in having one of the through lines with platforms either side.

Peterborough North station I remember as dark, busy and pretty conventional, with three through lines and an Up side bay. Our wartime and Christmas journeys involved very crowded trains with station staff struggling to get doors closed because of the mass of bodies, but, for me, these travels produced the consolation of time to admire the great main-line locomotives on Grantham shed when we changed trains there. I also remember Peterborough North for the rock cakes in the refreshment rooms, the colourful bookstall, the Nestlé's chocolate bar machine and one on which you could print a metal label (somewhat laboriously though). East seemed slightly more mysterious, for one neighbour was the dark waters of Stanground Pool where decaying old barges recalled the days of traffic barged in from the Fens for transfer to railway wagons. Woodston Wharf along the original London & Birmingham line was another thorn in the flesh of the LNER companies, which resented good business being syphoned off from stations in their territory.

Everything about the Peterborough area railways fascinated me, from the great complex of brickworks sidings to the south and east, to the vast New England marshalling sidings to the north; from the prestigious main-line expresses to the mixed services that linked the two stations; and from the great Spital coaling plant to the special locomotive visitors, including an LMS Beyer-Garratt giant.

With my Cambridge School Certificate safely achieved, I left Deacons Grammar School, surrendered to these early influences and applied to join the staff of the LNER with my first interview at Peterborough.

Today's Peterborough station profile is very different. The old North station has been replaced by a much-improved layout and the former restrictive curves it imposed on the main line have been swept away, but one old story still survives:

Too late a passenger realised that the train he was on did not stop at Peterborough North where even through services were forced to slow because of sharp curves through the station platforms.

He desperately needed to alight and resolved, as the train slowed, to leap out and hit the platform running to avoid falling over. This he did, but just as his feet touched the platform, a station inspector, with a mighty heave, pushed him back through the still open carriage door and remarked, 'You're OK now, Sir, but you nearly missed it!'

PASSENGER STATIONS AND GOODS DEPOTS 🖅

Live Chicks and Lyons Cakes

Monday, 29 October 1945 was a grey, damp day, but that could not diminish my excitement. I was about to embark on a railway career that was to last for twenty-eight years and then to continue that association with railways for many more. A little before, I had received a letter appointing me as a 'temporary probationary junior male clerk' on the London & North Eastern Railway and instructing me to report to St Neots station for my training. Weather unnoticed, I cycled to Peterborough North station, stored my machine in an old outbuilding of the adjacent Great Northern Hotel and crossed to the station entrance. Proudly displaying my privilege season ticket, I strutted along to the bay at the London end of the main Up platform and boarded my train. So taken was I with a sense of belonging that I stood for the whole of the six-stage journey in an empty guard's compartment trying to look as if I had business there.

Assigned by Class II station master Archie Mehew to the booking and parcels office, I learned how to issue the various types of ticket and to take money for things like 'Left Luggage' or 'Passengers Luggage in Advance'

St Neots station, rather smarter in appearance here than in its original form.

and how to account for it in the daily balance. Once I got the hang of it, this proved not too difficult since the 'value' items were all numbered in sequence and multiplying the difference between the day's opening and closing stock numbers by their value should equate to the cash collected. A bigger problem was the huge size of the forms on which all this was recorded. A skill one had to acquire quickly was using the ticket-dating machine, which could easily catch a dilatory thumb in its converging jaws if one was not quick enough to get it out of the way.

On a bad day it could take a long time to achieve a cash balance. Occasionally it just proved impossible and there was an official procedure for dealing with it. I was not aware of this and, consequently, when questioned by an auditor on one of their periodical visits, I naively told him that we put any surplus in our tea supplies tin. The senior of the three girls who manned the office and who had responsibility for instructing me looked aghast.

In a surprisingly short time I found myself able to hold the local train service and its main onward connections in my memory and to respond to train enquiries promptly. Somewhat more difficult was fathoming the big range of special tickets and fares for customers such as commercial travellers, many of whom were still, at that time, setting off with their suitcases of samples every Monday for a sales tour entirely by train. Groups such as blind people with attendants were entitled to fare concessions, while members of the armed forces, police or warders with prisoners and others in this sort of 'official' category usually presented a warrant in exchange for their journey ticket. All needed recording and processing.

A spell in the parcels office followed, sticking denominational stamps and destination/route labels onto items being despatched by train, or 'Ledger Labels' in the case of customers with an account. Incoming items, anything from chirping live chicks to Lyons cakes, had to be entered either on the counter sheets if being collected or on the carmen's sheets if to be delivered. The St Neots parcels delivery vehicle was a small 2-ton Bedford with no side windows, and when the driver left it outside to take his lunch in the porters' room I frequently took the opportunity to drive it down to the goods yard and back. He must have known but voiced no protest and I quickly got the hang of swinging the starting handle after it had clouted me a few times. Another salutary experience was travelling back to Peterborough in the evenings with relief lorry driver Arthur South. A group of us travelled in the front compartments of the front coach, as railwaymen always did, and I cajoled my way into the card school active there. No one took advantage of my obvious desire to be part of railway life, but sadly I had not learned enough from regularly being beaten at Solo by my father and paid out modestly and frequently for that failure.

My other extracurricular activity was (carefully) crossing the main line to visit the signal box, where I was generally made welcome and put to use sending bell signals and pulling levers under the very watchful eye of the man on duty. The St Neots patch was fairly straightforward with just Up and Down main and slow lines and connections between them, plus the lead into the dock, goods shed and goods yard. There was a great deal of passing traffic, with long coal trains trying to keep out of the way of the main-line expresses, the 'Parly' stopping trains, fast freights like the Aberdeen Meat special and local goods pickup services all adding to the variety. With the war barely over, all but a few of the locomotives were grimy and unkempt, but pride was just beginning to show again in the cleaning that had been done on some of the A3 and A4 Pacifics handling the prestige expresses. Not so fortunate were the Austerities, Moguls and 02 engines. They still laboured by in the clanking way that the intense pressures of wartime traffic had led to.

Rather Less Glamorous

Before moving to the goods office for my next training period, I had a week in a small room on the Up platform, learning that the main-line railways were major producers of grain sacks which we provided free to farmers sending their corn by rail. There was a whole system of accounting for these, raising charges for those not returned on time and arranging for damaged ones to be sent to the sack depot at Lincoln for repair. My instructor was a young woman who was married to a farmer and was well able to enlighten me as to some of the ways they had for avoiding their obligations. For some reason I recall that the clerical staff were obliged to use the nearby platform toilets, and each office had a special key to permit access without the customary penny for the door entry machine: a lofty privilege indeed.

In the goods office, Class IV chief clerk Joe Doncaster presided over a staff of one young man and three and a half women. The half was an attractive brunette whose sad-seeming half presence was due, I learned, to an unhappy liaison with an unavailable local innkeeper. They were all pleasant and helpful, the young man – Peter – introducing me to horse racing at the small Brampton Racecourse, where I managed a losing bet on every race, even the one with only three runners! My railway career was doing better than my gambling apprenticeship.

My first task was just addressing envelopes, not difficult for the GPO mail but less simple than I might have supposed for the internal railway correspondence, all of which was carried by train, duly marked OCS – On Company's Service. An effective address had to show not only the current railway concerned but also its pre-1923 group, thus Derby had to be Derby (Mid) unless it was for the LNER station there, when the address had to record Derby (Friargate) (GN). Things got even more complicated with a destination like Manchester with its dozens of stations and depots to choose from. However, in those days I learned quickly and could then move on to all the other goods traffic procedures, waybills, abstracts and summaries (for the revenue-division work of the Railway Clearing House), demurrage returns and so on. It all contributed to my successfully passing an examination in 'Goods Station Work and Accounts'.

44,000 Missing Sacks

In due course I was considered trained and needed to start earning my keep. Accordingly I was moved two stations along the line to Sandy, where the track layout was very different to the basic four through lines at St Neots. Sandy was a meeting point between the LNER main line and the LMS cross-country route from Bletchley, through Bedford (St Johns), to Cambridge. To accommodate the two routes in the space available, Sandy LNER had only Up and Down main lines through the station itself. The Up platform was, in fact, an island with its other face used by the LMS services to Bedford. The original LMS buildings were on the remaining platform used by trains to Cambridge, but were no longer in normal use as all functions were carried out by LNER staff.

The west–east LMS route from Bedford was single-track and crossed over the LNER via a skew overbridge to the north of the station, then dropping down past the dock siding to the platforms. My new location was in the adjacent and vacant LMS goods office and, with the small LMS signal box at the end of the joint platform only a few yards away, I had a good opportunity to add signalling a single-line section using tablet instruments to my understanding of operating procedures. Another attraction was a small mobile canteen left over from the days of wartime troop interchange, but still dispensing tea, cakes and sandwiches.

My new task was not exactly front-line railway activity. Local farmers had managed to spirit out of the system some 44,000 grain sacks and it was my task to try either to get them back or to exact payment for their loss or detention. It called for guile and perseverance, but I did get the total of errant sacks halved before being required to move on.

While at Sandy I had the opportunity to understand the goods activity in the Down side LNER yard and shed (and to get to know a young lady clerk in the office who was later to become my wife). The fertile land of the area was the home of a number of market gardening businesses, most of which used the railway for much of their produce. Lorries and carts would arrive with boxes and crates of various vegetables from early afternoon onwards, which needed to be weighed full and later empty to arrive at the chargeable weight of what was then loaded into the Vanfit wagons. Attached to the Class C express fully-braked freight trains, along with similar loadings from Biggleswade and Langford Sidings, the produce would be speeded to the London and provincial markets. Growers, of course, wanted to go on picking until the latest possible moment, but demanded early and punctual market delivery to be sure of the best prices, so great haste was always the order of the day.

Before I left Sandy I had been loaned for a week to nearby LMS Blunham and managed to deal with its passenger business without too much difficulty. I had also managed to collect my first reprimand, not a formal one, just a strong suggestion that a letter to the district office at Leicester expressing my view on something I perceived as nonsense would have been better signed by someone more senior!

Dead Rabbits Smell

With hindsight I have come to believe that the closure of the Bletchley–Cambridge route was short-sighted, albeit understandable in the political and financial climate of the time. The same, I think, might also be said about the next route on which I worked. I was sent to Littleworth station, near Spalding, where the line then carried quite a good service from London via Peterborough and then on to Boston, Louth and Grimsby. At the time, the finances of the East Lincs line route did not match up to Beeching criteria but any transport planner today might see the strategic position rather differently. That being as it may, I did not enjoy my short time at Littleworth, partly due to the confusion of having to catch an early train there one day and a much later one the next, and partly due to the sarcastic Yorkshire station master whose enthusiasm for the station's extensive but smelly freight despatches of dead rabbits I could not fully match.

Happily, my stay at Littleworth was short, and when my father secured a promotion to a post in the Norwich district, the family moved to Norwich and I duly went with them to work in that area.

Cider and Cockles

Before being summoned for National Service I was to work at some twelve locations in the Norwich district and learn to love the city, the county and its proud, warm people. Another of the by-products was that I became a regular visitor to The Firs speedway stadium to delight in the thrills of the roaring bikes and accept my obligatory covering of the ash they threw up from the track. I also became a lifelong supporter of Norwich City Football Club, 'the Canaries', and cheered along with thousands of others, especially on the occasion when the popular goalkeeper, Ken Nethercott, lost his shorts.

On the more serious front of my railway career, my first posting was to Eccles Road, a small station between Norwich and Ely, and on what was then a main line to Cambridge and London, and to the Midlands via Peterborough. Apart from serving the small township of Banham and a local cider-making company, it was not a busy place and I was not really needed, as the severe, middle-aged lady incumbent of the small platform office made clear. I was there to learn to use the single-needle electric telegraph system, which was the main means of communication between places on the former Great Eastern Railway system and was housed in booking offices rather than in the signal box, as was the case on the old Great Northern lines. So we had a two-faced teaching machine and sent one another stiff messages in Morse code across the 18 inches between us. The hub of the local system was at Norwich, where there was a telegraph office on the station from which the public could send messages.

The chief staff clerk of the Norwich district was Cyril Birkett, a shrewd and likeable man dedicated to his work and keen to secure the development of the staff under his control. Resulting from this commitment, I was given a 'summer relief' position which would widen my experience as a result of being placed wherever there was a need, not to mention giving me the useful financial dividend of being entitled to expenses when away from my Norwich home station.

Off I went to tackle the first challenge of being considered competent in station commercial matters and procedures. The location was Wells-next-the-Sea, then Wells-on-Sea before the purists started to fret over the fact of its separation from open water by the long channel to the town's harbour.

A line curved round the town from the quayside to the modest terminal station used by the passenger services on the line to Norwich via Dereham and west to join the Hunstanton–King's Lynn line at Heacham. The latter was notorious in that its electric telegraph took up an unsolicited chatter of its own when there was the slightest breeze to stimulate the trackside wires. This was somewhat frustrating to the local users, myself included.

The passenger and parcels business at Wells was of the run-of-the-mill variety except for the cockles, harvested by the local fishing fleet and then demanding urgent despatch when brought into our parcels office. The dozens of small hessian bags, soggy with salt water, dripped everywhere. Their tie-on labels got wet and consistently refused to accept the parcels stamps that had to be glued on. But we managed somehow and dashed off along the platform, hauling clumsily laden parcels trolleys in order to catch the next available train and earn the disapproval of a guard whose brake compartment soon became soggy and smelly too.

A notable feature of this end of the line was the flow of Catholic pilgrims to the famous shrine at Walsingham, many of them arriving and departing via the tiny halt on the single-line section south from Wells to Fakenham.

As it turned out, Fakenham was to be my next appointment, as I was sent there to cover the temporary absence of the chief booking clerk. It came as something of a shock to find that my early and late turn clerks were even younger than I was and that neither had any idea how to work the single-needle system. This task accordingly fell to me, causing some frustration among the expert Morse senders at Norwich, especially as they could be halted by just holding the needle over until calm returned.

My route to and from work at this time was single at the northern end, served a green and fertile area of Norfolk, and provided goods traffic from various maltings and granaries together with a considerable flow of milk. Wells at one time was, in fact, the biggest of the country's malt exporters with six maltings sending out ship cargoes, not only to London and other British ports but also to Holland and Ireland.

From a junction at County School ran a meandering single line eastwards to join the Norwich–Cromer line at Wroxham. It carried a respectable Norwich–Dereham passenger service, taking around an hour and a half for the 38.5-mile journey. Unsurprisingly, railwaymen referred to this as 'Round the World' and I believe that at least one of the quieter stations had a station master post rated only as Class VI, when the normal lowest grade was Class V. I was later to work at one of the stations at the eastern end, Coltishall, which did not prove unduly taxing. Understandably, the line did not survive the closure years, but it later found a new lease of life as the narrow-gauge Bure Valley Railway, running some way out from Coltishall.

The passenger trains on the Wells line and its link from Dereham via Swaffham to King's Lynn were typical of that period between the end of the war and the end of the LNER. The motive power was mainly D16 'Claud' 4-4-0s, generally grimy and a bit run down, but perfectly capable of keeping time with the usual four-coach set of handed-down BK and BCK compartment coaches. Other locomotive types appeared from time to time, especially 0-6-0s and E3 2-4-0s, but it was a fairly routine existence. In a grand railway plan that was visionary rather than finance-controlled, these lines to King's Lynn and Wells would still be there, but at least a part still thrives as the Mid-Norfolk heritage line.

The East Anglian Herring Season

I was to return to the Wells line later, but not before putting in a stint at Norwich Thorpe parcels office, a very routine job and one that deprived me of my modest lunchtime expenses allowance, since it was my 'home station'. Then came a very exciting and colourful period when I was sent to Lowestoft to supplement the staff needed to deal with the huge volume of fish traffic despatched by rail during the East Anglian herring season. This was the time when the herring shoals had moved south down the coast from Scotland and all the attendant fishing fleet paraphernalia had moved down with them, not just trawlers and drifters, but salesmen, handlers, fishergirls and others. With the local vessels joining in the daily sea harvesting and bringing their bounty back to the Lowestoft fish market, a hectic period of rail office and operating activity was sure to follow.

Early on the appointed morning I walked onto Platform 5 at Norwich Thorpe station to take the all-stations train to Lowestoft. It consisted of a string of ancient coaches, all having reached the lowest rung on their active existence and not one matching the roof line of its neighbour. I chose an ex-NER non-corridor vehicle, one with the tiny door handles that the company seemed to favour.

After the short walk from the Lowestoft terminal station to the goods office I learned that the main element of this new experience was to be periods of frantic waybilling of the consignments of boxed herrings rushed in from the fish market and loaded onto the fish vans of the Class C express freight services to London. Such hasty scribbling did little for the elegance of my handwriting but, happily, there were often periods when I could visit the fish market and enjoy the quite unforgettable sight of countless trawlers and drifters appearing out of a late autumn mist to squeeze adroitly into a seemingly impossible space somewhere along the already-crowded quays. Crans of glittering herrings were everywhere being slung ashore to be boxed, iced and labelled, and then laid out for the army of buyers who did their business in a language largely unintelligible to the uninformed observer, even with gestures. Lots were sold and cleared, and all the time information was circulating about the size of the various catches, important to the pride and price ranking of the skippers.

A piece of prime fish for supper easily and cheaply acquired, I would make my way back to the modest goods office along Commercial Road. As often as not it was foggy and this backdrop made the long line of stalls of the fishergirls – lit by their peculiar oil lanterns, busy with their dexterous fingers and noisy with their constant banter – an amazing adjunct to the activity I had seen earlier at the dock.

A Lost Train

National Service was looming but I had one more placement before being called up. This was back to the Wells line at Hardingham, a pretty ordinary place with a few passengers, parcels and the odd goods consignment, mainly inwards coal. Another skill had to be acquired, though: that of managing the Tilley lamps, which gave brilliant illumination when they were in good fettle and needed much humouring at other times. In the daily routine of small station life at the end of 1946, little did I suspect what lay ahead.

It started to snow. And went on snowing until the depth had reached a point where I doubted getting back to Norwich. We heard that a train had been stranded north of Dereham, but a substitute service was to be worked south from Dereham with whatever locomotive and stock could be found there. Using it and picking up another scratch service at Wymondham, I finally got home on that first and worst day and, miraculously, was able to get back to work again the following morning. Overnight the stranded train had been relieved of its passengers and was apparently being dug out with the help of Italian prisoners of war who had not yet returned to their sunnier climes.

And then the snow melted. The whole distance from Hardingham to the junction at Wymondham and then through Hetherset to Norwich featured bridges spanning many normally small and quiet streams, but as I travelled home when the thaw started the angry waters rushing through these could be heard in the darkness and despite the noise of the carriage. At one period the main line out to Ely had to be closed, and when I used it shortly after reopening it was my first such experience. Looking from a railway carriage at a vast expanse of water either side of the line, with little in the way of other objects – the condition that existed on the stretch through Lakenheath and Shippea Hill – was quite eerie.

On Her Majesty's Service

My call-up papers duly arrived and it was to be two and a half years before Her Majesty released me to return to railway service. I made a few train journeys in that time, starting with one from Padgate to West Kirby via Helsby and Hooton, a journey where we were locked in to prevent defections. After the rather tough ordeal of basic training had been successfully completed came various postings and the regular weekend passes that went with being a fully enrolled member of the Royal Air Force (RAF). From No. 4 Bomber Group headquarters Marham to my home in Norwich just meant getting to Narborough & Pentney station, but the journey to or from my fiancée's home in Bedfordshire was slightly more complicated. Staying until the last possible moment meant a night on Peterborough North station and the early meandering M&GN route to King's Lynn. Leaving at an earlier time permitted a journey back from Sandy to Cambridge and thence forward to Downham Market or King's Lynn, where two local omnibus services provided a link to our camp. They used different types of coach, followed different routes and were madly competitive.

The occasional travel warrant helped with the cost of taking leave and I continued to be entitled to privilege tickets, and also to say 'OCS' (On Company's Service) when ordering a cup of tea in a station refreshment room and getting it for a penny less than non-railway people!

BIGGLESWADE STATION BOOKING OFFICE 🏃

The Fire Hogger

After demobilisation from the RAF in 1949, I married the girl I had first met at Sandy station. The ceremony took place in a small Bedfordshire village chapel where the previous entry in the register was my bride's christening! A number of detonators in front of our train marked our

The frontage of Biggleswade station where the entrance doors led to a traditional booking office, with parcels office beyond, and footbridge to the lower-level island platforms. The porters' and lamp rooms were at the far end.

departure for the honeymoon. Happily, we were able to rent a small detached house from a family member at the tiny settlement of Seddington on the Great North Road.

To accommodate my new status I was permitted to resume my railway service in a Class V clerk position in Biggleswade booking office, a few miles' cycle ride away from our new, sparsely furnished, home. The establishment was for two such clerks and a Class IV chief clerk. A week's pay for the former position was £5 6s 9d in return for working six early or late turns and alternate Sundays. The booking office was open from 6 a.m. to 9 p.m. and prompt morning arrival was essential if the workmen were to get the workmen's tickets they were entitled to on the first train. Hitchin would complain bitterly if they had to issue excess tickets because Biggleswade booking office was not opened on time. My cycle ride from Seddington was sometimes a bit frantic!

A small, stooped man called Harry Holroyd occupied the Class IV position, but did not get on well with Class I Station Master Soames, a brusque and florid East Anglian. Harry loved warmth and sat with his back close to the office fire, which my opposite number and I often built up to the point where it caused the chair varnish to bubble, but we could never shift him. Offered a large note for a short journey ticket, he enquired of one passenger, 'Do you think I've got the Bank of England in here?' and then scurried to lock the office door when the disgruntled individual tried to get at him with menacing intent. The attitude must have been catching, for I got a reproof from the District Goods & Passenger Manager's Office (DG&PMO) at Peterborough for being less than helpful to one particularly arrogant passenger. Others thought better of us and one regular season ticket holder rewarded our initiative in getting a local garage to change the flat tyres on his parked car before he arrived back at the station. One year our Christmas boxes included a bag of Brussels sprouts and dead poultry; it was just the way things were in a community dominated by the market gardening that still produced a great deal of traffic for the goods yard, despite the growing advances of road competition.

A parcels office was included with the booking office in the street-level station building at Biggleswade, a footbridge then leading to the two island platforms. The prestige main-line trains sped through the station on the Up and Down fast lines, headed by locomotives of the various Pacific classes, including the streamlined A4s. Locals – which we called 'Parlys' – tended to have V2 Class 2-6-2 motive power with a few 2-6-0s, L1 tanks, etc. Coal trains were a regular sight and the goods yard had calls by the Class C express freight services which conveyed local produce loadings to London and provincial centres. The passenger clientele had no pattern except for a few regulars on the morning fast service to London and the 'Mark Lane' return working in the evening.

The job was varied and interesting, and embraced not only the booking office work but also collecting tickets and getting involved with pretty well anything that needed doing, giving a hand to load or unload a guard's van, sheeting out parcels for delivery and so on. It was to serve me well enough for a couple of years until ambition and our parlous finances prompted more interest in the regular vacancy lists that circulated. The result was leaving rural East Bedfordshire behind for the very different atmosphere of London.

I was able to continue as a Methodist local preacher, making appearances in small village chapels where the elders clung to a pattern that had been unchanged for decades – including marked fidgeting if the sermon exceeded twenty minutes! Also continuing was the attempt at mushroom growing and mass production of carrots on an allotment, in the vain hope of earning money to supplement our happy but spartan living.

JOINT ROAD/RAIL OFFICE, FINSBURY PARK ☞

Off to 'The Smoke'

In the early 1950s I was successful in securing promotion to a Class IV position in this office, an out-based activity of the two Eastern Region (ER) London goods managers (City and Suburban). Its role was to organise the railway opposition to applications for road haulage A and B licences in accordance with the Road and Rail Traffic Act of 1933. The office was located in a first-floor room above The Silver Bullet pub opposite Finsbury Park station, a facility to which we had recourse from time to time. Staffing comprised Special Class B Tom Gregory (nominally in charge but rarely in the office), Class II FT Justice (called 'Jimmy' because we never knew what the FT stood for), myself, John Moody and typist Christine Sharp. John kept the records, my job was to prepare the briefs for our representatives appearing to oppose licence applications, and Jim both made the decisions about which cases to contest and appeared in support of our counsel in the Traffic Court.

In Court

The work involved scrutiny of the booklets of 'Applications & Decisions' issued by the Metropolitan Traffic Commissioner to decide which requests for a new or extended licence were prejudicial to railway interests. In such cases a formal objection was lodged and the merit of the case then argued before the commissioner in a legal format and by the barrister or other advocate briefed by the objector. It was my job to prepare such briefs, embodying the haulier's history, railway facilities to carry the traffic under notice, existing rail traffic at risk and other relevant information. Jim Justice normally carried out the in-court support and appeared as a rail witness as necessary, although I undertook this task when he was unavailable. It was not something to be treated lightly, for being the subject of cross-examination by an astute barrister could be pretty daunting.

One of my routes to court involved a tram journey and I rather enjoyed the dip and twist bits at Holborn Kingsway, especially when viewed from a front seat on the top deck. There were also a few lighter moments amid the court proceedings. One such occurred when a farmer seeking to carry neighbours' sugar beet to Felstead factory was asked what the distance was from his farm 'as the crow flies', so that this could be embodied in his licence conditions. He replied, 'I don't know, Your Honour, I've never done it that way!' At the other extreme the clash of barristers in a major case could be quite exciting to witness.

Commuting Studies

To get to work I left Sandy about 8.15 each morning, arriving at Finsbury Park at 9.15 a.m. after a journey calling at all stations to Hatfield and then Potters Bar. On the whole timekeeping was good, even when work began on adding a second tunnel at the Hadley Wood bottleneck. The evening return was usually on the 6 p.m. from Finsbury Park, which was double-headed (by Class B1 and Claud locos in the main) as far as Hitchin, where the Cambridge portion was taken forward by the train engine (while I visited the Refreshment Room) and then the Peterborough portion by the pilot. When Tom Gregory was in a good mood I got to go home on the 4.10 p.m. from King's Cross, always known as the 'Mark Lane', something to do with its market clientele.

In those days I had to work alternate Saturdays and, with Jim and John respectively Tottenham and Arsenal supporters, often found myself at one or other of the respective grounds after the morning's work, thankful always for the crush barriers that ensured some degree of comfort and safety. I had decided to seek Institute of Transport qualifications, the studies for which had, of necessity, to be by correspondence course. My commuter train journeys were ideal for this purpose except that, in the winter months, trying to absorb information was not helped by broken train heating pipes and, sometimes, ice coating the *inside* of the train windows.

The Institute branch to which I was allocated held its meetings at The University Arms in Cambridge and I was fortunate in finding someone who would give me a lift there and back. The lectures I attended doubtless made their contribution to my successful passing of the first batch of six examinations and duly becoming a graduate of the Institute. Whether the discussion in our regular pub of call on the way home helped, I know not, but it was certainly stimulating.

In June 1951, I took and passed an examination, at the LSE I think, in the 'Law Relating to the Conveyance of Goods and Passengers by Railway' and in April 1953 an examination in 'Goods Terminal and Cartage Working'.

Then, in May 1953, I passed the six Institute of Transport subjects that qualified me for associate membership and could now sport the post-nominal AMInstT, which I did with a certain amount of pride, satisfaction and relief. On the way to one examination the piston rod fell from our L1 train locomotive just outside King's Cross, throwing ballast through the window of my compartment and considerably worsening my exam nerves!

I was beginning to feel that my studies and experience ought to be moving me forward on the promotional ladder and helping with the family income, especially as my son Ian had been born in 1950. I tried for a post in the district superintendent's office at Knebworth, but was told by the forthright district operating superintendent Bill Green that 'You will not get this job; do you no good if you did.' Thus was I saved from the drudgery of examining guards' journals. Thankfully, I also failed to get a job on the medical officer's staff, for that would have been another career tributary.

At this stage I was still thinking in terms of the wider transport world and responded to advertising by SPD, Richard Thomas & Baldwins and even an Ilford laundry that wanted someone to run its fleet of delivery vans. Unilever was seeking transport trainees and the series of interviews with them included a day with the Tavistock Institute of Human Relations staff when, as I remember it, we had to debate the ethics of opening a brewery in some less-developed society overseas. I failed at the last hurdle to get one of these posts and was offered a job in SPD instead, but I declined. Nor did I accept the offer made by Richard Thomas & Baldwin – I often wonder where a different decision in either of these cases might have led.

However, at last I broke out of the road-licensing backwater after an interview for a temporary Class III post at Norwich, to which I was transferred on 10 May 1954.

CANVASSING AND DEVELOPMENT SECTION, NORWICH 🖎

This was a passenger and freight commercial section reporting to the district passenger manager and to G.G. Goodings, who then occupied an experimental post as area freight manager, supposedly coordinating road and rail goods haulage activities. I never saw any evidence that this was working and from my own experience of British Road Services in the previous post I could not see how it would. Run by Freddie Cobb and housed in the Thorpe station offices, the section was also the base for the district commercial representatives, including the livestock representative who was deeply involved in things like the movement of Irish cattle to the Acle marshes for fattening. Among other things, the section was responsible for the complex problems of getting traffic – machinery, exhibits, livestock and equipment – to and from the Royal Norfolk Show: a lesson in complex logistics.

Humour Competitions

My temporary Class III post involved supporting the reps in their traffic-securing activities, recording and reporting results and, oddly, prosecuting objections to public service vehicle (PSV) road licence applications, which entailed occasional visits to the traffic court in Cambridge and liaison with the Eastern Counties Omnibus Company. Lunches with the traffic court group in a local hostelry were wont to turn into memorable joke-telling sessions!

It was pleasant to be back in Norwich again and to enjoy the benefits of 'lodging' with my parents. The office was a good one and a bonus was a view over the busy station where Ely line trains generally used Platform 1, the services on the Ipswich main line Platforms 2 and 3, and the coastal routes Platforms 4 and 5. At weekends, either I would go back to my home at Seddington or Sheila would come to Norwich. But this was always a temporary posting and I still felt an urge to be more involved in the practicalities of railway traffic movement. An abortive interview in July 1954 for a permanent Class III post in the Claims Section at Cambridge was then followed by a successful one in September for a Class III Cartage & Terminals job at Gordon Hill, Enfield.

GENERAL SECTION, DISTRICT GOODS MANAGER'S OFFICE, GORDON HILL 📧

A Busy Freight District

On 4 October 1954, I took up the Class III post in charge of the Cartage & Terminals subsection of the office of the District Goods Manager (London Suburban). The office itself could hardly be described as palatial, just a wartime wooden building located on the Great Northern Athletic Association sports ground near Gordon Hill station in north Enfield. It was mostly open plan with a tiny switchboard in one corner and decidedly ancient heating. E.O. Lloyd was the district goods manager, presenting as rather austere and conscious of his position. Ted Waller, his assistant – formerly goods agent at King's Cross – was decidedly more human, while Herbert Smith, the 'assistant to', could be avuncular on occasions.

The territory covered the outer Eastern Region rail routes north and east of London with important goods traffic railheads at Romford, Ponders End, Waltham Cross, Broxbourne, Harlow, Bishops Stortford and Welwyn Garden City. It contained a lot of rail activity with several very significant locations and important traffics such as that to the coal concentration depot at the original station at Enfield Chase and the Lea Valley furniture industry, and also a variety of private sidings. The busy functional part was leavened by three single-line branches off the GNR main line and the wandering rural route out to Buntingford, well loved by film producers.

This was a time of considerable change. On a personal level, Sheila and I had agreed that this move to London was necessary for my advancement and our reaching a better degree of solvency and hopes of a more normal home life. We duly set about the daunting task of finding a new home and of arranging a mortgage for it, the first step on the property ladder. A few months later we left behind our Bedfordshire hamlet of half a dozen houses to move to the outskirts of Enfield and set about slowly furnishing our new home. Then came the birth of our second son, Richard, earlier than expected and causing a few anxious moments at first.

Until we moved I had been in lodgings at Palmers Green, overfed by the jolly wife of a printworker, but now I had to tackle all the responsibilities of gardening, house maintenance and the like.

On a wider front, the rail industry as a whole was at last producing a small 'profit', but had never fully recovered from the years of war and was still rooted in past equipment, practices and thinking. The announcement of the 1954 Modernisation Plan held the high promise of a new era that, in the event, was not to be realised, largely because much of the investment proved less than far sighted.

The Gordon Hill office had four main sections: Staff, Development/Works, Claims and General. Cyril Scarrow was in charge of the latter with Bill Hall as his deputy. Stan Morgan was the wagon control clerk and Maurice Gershon headed the movements subsection. My own subsection had George Burrows to look after terminal matters (including cost-of-handling returns), Bill Bright covering cartage (including scrutiny of drivers' log sheets), Ted Baker and myself. There were at my disposal two inspectors,

Dave McPhee and Dick Hayden, and three relief drivers using a 4-ton rigid vehicle, a 3-ton three-wheel Scammell articulated vehicle and a 6-ton Bedford artic, the last two with spare trailers of various types. We also had two mobile cranes, a rigid 3-ton Jumbo and a Walker lorry-mounted crane which could lift 6 tons when the outriggers were used.

Lorries, Cranes and Handling Staff

All the major freight depots in our area had sizeable lorry fleets plus cranes and other equipment, and dealt with a huge range of goods. This was the first time I had been in charge of other people and there was an initial period of coolness from them while they weighed me up, and partly because their own hopes of getting the job had not been realised. The two inspectors were very knowledgeable but vastly different, Dick a grizzled, experienced veteran, and Dave a younger man more willing to seek novel solutions. Both more than proved their worth, Dave McPhee being a wizard with the complicated business of dealing with out-of-gauge loads. These were surprisingly numerous and the first move was always to check their dimensions against the loading gauge chart. One look at this showed an astonishing lack of any semblance of standardised track profiles among the original railway companies.

Ted Baker was likeable but given to regular safaris round the office carrying a small suitcase. Was this full of important papers, I wondered, and asked, 'Ted, what's in the case?'

'Just personal stuff, Boss.'

When I insisted on it being shown, the suitcase turned out to contain confectionery which he touted around for a small supplement to his salary!

'Fine, but the job comes first,' I stipulated, having no wish to alienate the whole office in my first couple of weeks by cutting off their chocolate supply.

My immediate boss was Cyril Scarrow, a likeable and able older man who, it was rumoured, filled up his petrol lighter with railway fuel, a rumour made believable by the smoke stain sometimes to be seen on his forehead. Stan Morgan was an avid Goons fan and had a tendency to undertake normal office communication in an excellent imitation of Bluebottle or the 'Famous Eccles'. Despite these small foibles, all of us, I believe, did our job conscientiously and well.

My responsibility covered station and depot terminal performance and was to ensure the adequacy, deployment and efficiency of the district's extensive collection, handling and delivery facilities, and the fixed and mobile cranage capacity. The routine of controlling the work of goods stations and depots was part of every day, but a day without some crisis or other was rare – extra traffic had been sprung on us, a driver had not turned up for work, a crane had broken down, and so on.

Always Something Different

In addition to routine traffic, which included heavy market garden produce forwardings from the Lea Valley, we handled large amounts of round timber through Ware station and a surprising variety of both the out-of-gauge and abnormal loads. The latter included delivery of some 60ft rails which we managed to move through Barking on the 6-ton Bedford by building a trailer cradle and putting ballast blocks on the tractor. During the 1955 strike by the Associated Society of Locomotive Engineers and Firemen (ASLE&F) we even arranged for relief driver Vic Groves to run the 3-ton, three-wheel articulated unit and trailer as far as Edinburgh as part of the effort to keep urgent traffic moving. Driving that sort of vehicle that sort of distance took some doing, but Vic seemed to manage it cheerfully. A few of us got a special commendation for the hours and effort we put in then.

Unusual circumstances like this were fairly common and we normally just got on and handled them, but one job that did cause extra serious thought was a request via the station master at Bishop Stortford. He presented it in a way calculated to shock: 'We've been asked to help in excavating the skeleton of a Roman soldier.'

Stunned silence at my end. I had become used to finding novel solutions for unusual handling problems, but this was a new one.

'Sorry,' came the follow-up. 'I couldn't help creating some mild consternation in district office. They only want to hire our crane and a driver.'

'OK,' said I, seeing some useful publicity in the offing, 'but for heaven's sake don't drop him.'

Thankfully all went well. We were well paid and got some flattering column inches.

Another occasion that tested us was one that still sticks in my mind. It started with advices coming in of huge consignments of cattle requiring unloading, then of a cartage vehicle overturning and, finally, of complications in unloading a circus train. At one time there seemed to be assorted loose animals running free in half our biggest goods depots! It is in times of crisis that railways and railwaymen show their calibre and this was no exception.

Sidelines

Early in 1955 came a restructuring of the clerical grades – which put the whole office on tenterhooks – and with it my 'assimilation' into Class II. The extra £60 a year enabled us to convert our house mortgage to a 'With Profits' basis, which turned out to be an astute move. As a member of the Eastern Region Staff Railway Society (ERSRS), I somehow got elected in 1956 as delegate to the British Railways Staff Association's area conference, held at Southend in the April.

A rather different affair around the same time was an ERSRS visit to Tilmanstone colliery. This Kent pit was deep, hot and wet, causing its miners to wear as little as possible! I did manage to mine a small lump of coal as a keepsake but would definitely not have wanted to do it for a living. The cement works at Cliffe was another venue we visited, memorable for being able to look into a kiln operating at 1,000°F.

A Landmark Decision

Already an associate member of the Institute of Transport, I continued my studies and further examinations brought me full membership, a satisfying moment after several years of effort. I also added two successful signalling examinations to the internal qualifications I already had in station working. If and where we should go next was something Sheila and I had to think about very carefully when the information about traffic apprentice appointments came out. I was 26 and it was now or never. Selection would mean a lot of sacrifices, hard work and up to three years of me being away from home. We decided in the end to go for it if I passed the preliminary examination. In May 1956 I did, then survived the subsequent Regional and British Transport Commission (BTC) interviews to be summoned, finally, into the 'guvnor's' office in mid-November and told I had secured one of the coveted places and would start training on the last day of the year at a salary of £641 p.a.

I had a few weeks as acting Class I deputy on the General Section to cover a temporary vacancy and then said farewell to my colleagues, many of whom had become close friends. The usual pleasant family Christmas contained an element of wondering what the coming year would bring. One thing was for sure. We knew that a major change in our lives now lay ahead.

BRITISH TRANSPORT COMMISSION

C. K. BIRD
General Manager

A. J. WHITE
Assistant General Manager

Telephone
BISHOPSGATE 7600
Ext. 2284

Telegraphic Address
MANAGER EASTLIN LONDON

BRITISH RAILWAYS

GENERAL MANAGER
EASTERN REGION
LIVERPOOL STREET STATION
LONDON, E.C.2

PERSONAL

12th November 1956

G.4961/16

Mr. G. Body,
District Goods Manager's Office,
GORDON HILL

Dear Sir,

EXAMINATION FOR TRAFFIC APPRENTICESHIPS
16th May 1956

I am pleased to advise you that following your interview with the Central Selection Committee at British
Transport Commission Headquarters on 31st October, you have
secured an appointment as a Traffic Apprentice and I
congratulate you on your success. I hope to see you before
you commence your training, which will be given in the
Eastern Region.

In accordance with the salary scales at present in
operation for Traffic Apprentices during their training,
you will be paid as under :-

	£
1st year	642 per annum
2nd year	669 per annum
3rd year	696 per annum.

Yours faithfully,

CK Bird

The letter that heralded a complete change in a railway career, signed, oddly, by a man from the same remote Lincolnshire village as Geoff Body's father.

TRAFFIC APPRENTICE TRAINING AT SPALDING

And so I found myself on the last day of 1956 travelling on a morning train from King's Cross to Peterborough, thinking about what lay ahead and very unsure of how people would treat me and how I should relate to them. It seemed odd to be walking from North station to the old, grey GNR offices which I had first visited seventeen years ago, seeking entry to the same industry that was now going to train me for higher management. I was to be seen by the district goods and passenger manager (DG&PM) before making my way to my first training location at Spalding.

'Now, about your Spalding report,' concluded the DG&PM after a few fairly predictable sentiments of welcome, explanation and guidance. 'The Traffic Apprentice Committee will want to know what you have learned and won't be interested in minor local matters.'

This, I thought, was undoubtedly true, but was also a veiled hint not to expose any shortcomings that might reflect on the district office administration. Nodding wisely, I took my leave and continued on to Spalding, where Goods Agent Hawkes gave me a warm welcome and personally delivered me to the lodgings which had been arranged by my church at home.

The first day of training was spent in the goods yard, much of it in such a major downpour that I had to pop into town and buy some heavy-duty rainwear from my woefully slender purse. The rest of the week followed the same pattern but with the weather improving and my feet getting more sore. Especially interesting was a tour of the British Sugar Corporation sidings, served by the yard pilot, and attendance at a flower auction, Spalding being the centre of a large flower-growing area and the growers presenting their crops and expected crops to an army of buyers and wholesalers.

Excluding the five supervisors, half of the total goods yard outdoor staff were road motor drivers, operating ten vehicles on ten rounds, and my next week until the Friday was spent travelling with them. Friday was devoted to a meeting with the main Traffic Apprentice (TA) Committee, at which I received details of my full two-and-a-half-year programme. 'Not too bad at all,' my diary records.

Thus my time in Spalding Goods continued, the task of understanding its operation leavened by events like a visit to the sale of 450 Irish cattle, getting involved in the unloading of some of them and visiting the coal handling depot at St John's Road.

The parcels, booking, station master's and telegraph office periods were equally interesting, in both administrative and practical terms. There was a great deal going on, with a lot of passenger travel on the three routes making junction at Spalding, four parcels trains calling to bring inwards parcels and clear the considerable outwards business, a station siding for the box vans used to carry flowers, and 400 messages a day through the telegraph office.

On top of all this was the thirteen-siding marshalling yard for dealing with a variety of services for Lincolnshire vegetable traffic, wagons exchanged to and from the M&GN and various local train movements. The yard had a staff of seventeen and used three pilot locomotives – a 204hp diesel shunter and two J Class steam locomotives. I had some time in each of Spalding's three signal boxes and then had a day with District Inspector Raines inspecting the three at Sleaford.

Home Comforts

Spalding operated local freight trips to link with the longer-distance services calling there. One took me out to Holbeach and back, and a second to Billingborough at the end of the truncated Bourne–Sleaford line. On that day there were wagons to be detached at most of the stations en route to Bourne where the engine ran round, and again on the second leg. This

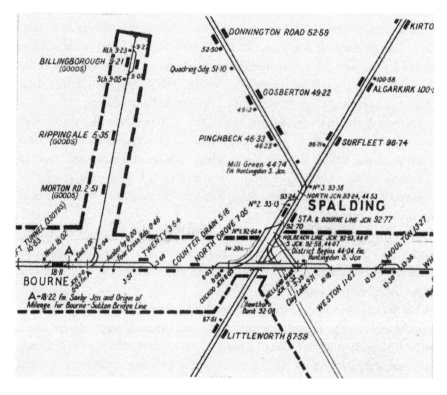

Spalding was once a busy and important railway junction.

occupied two hours, during which time the guard had plenty to do in shunting and attending to the level crossings. This was a permanent roster for him and, since he had the same brake van allocated for every trip, he had transformed it into a cosy kind of gypsy caravan. There was a gun rack, another for his pipes, curtains at the windows and quite a nice teapot and crockery. Shades of a long-gone era hanging on, I thought, but I saw no reason to expose something pretty harmless and likely soon to end anyway. Doubtless those who needed to turn a blind eye could rely on a gift of game garnered from the lineside.

Before making my farewells at Spalding I had a few days away, first in London combining advice from Operating Superintendent Gerry Fiennes on my forthcoming training period at Whitemoor, then a day in Liverpool Street booking office – quite an eye-opener – followed by attendance at a Ministry of Transport railway accident inquiry at Leicester.

AT WHITEMOOR MARSHALLING YARD

On Monday, 4 March, I set off for Whitemoor Yard by way of the District Office at Cambridge, where I had a friendly introductory session with the district operating superintendent, Harry Crosthwaite. Moving on to March and a long walk from the station to the Whitemoor yard offices, I was again welcomed, this time by the yard master, Harry Onyon, and then handed over to the assistant yard master, Bobby McKinnon, for a tour of the huge marshalling yard complex. When, exhausted, I finally got to my new digs, it was to be greeted with a somewhat frosty reception. Apparently the two elderly spinsters who owned the rambling Victorian house had been strong-armed by their church minister into taking me and now feared for their lives and virtue.

I endured my off-duty discomfort until the end of that first week and then moved to a happier situation, staying with the Brands, a March depot engine driver and his wife. I had also acquired a bicycle, an absolute essential for reaching some of the far corners of the Whitemoor 'estate'. This stretched for nearly 2 miles north from March along either side of the Great Northern and Great Eastern (GN&GE) joint line towards Spalding, and had grown and changed from its origins in 1929 until its 100 miles of track was handling nearly 5,000 wagons a day at the time I was there. From north to south the Up side had reception sidings leading to the hump and then the control tower, retarders, sorting and departure sidings, and it was the same on the Down, except that departures from there left straight from the sorting sidings. The small Norwood 'knuckle' yard dealt with both odds and ends and urgent wagons, while scattered around the complex were the signal boxes, Up and Down transit sheds, carriage and wagon sidings plus a brake van 'kip' and an engine release road on the Up side.

Humping

Two Class 08 diesel shunters were allocated to each hump, Norwood had its own pilot and there were six more for 'pushing down' in the sorting sidings and for yard-to-yard transfers. There was an assistant yard master for each shift and a huge complement of inspectors, head shunters, shunters, wagon chasers and various technical staff. The function of the yard was to marshal the inwards traffic from the north via the GN&GE joint line and the other routes, for its onward movement, especially towards London and East Anglia. A lot of empties and a great deal of agricultural produce went in the reverse directions.

The Whitemoor Up hump signal is off as a single wagon 'cut' starts the descent towards the points and retarders that precede the sorting sidings.

This was not quite as straightforward as it might seem, for inevitably all sorts of non-standard movements had to be dealt with, ranging from the urgent and hectic forwardings of perishable Lincolnshire fruit in season to wagons which could not pass through the retarders. This latter category included ferry wagons when the retarder grip would shear the bolts off their wheels and heavy steel-carrying wagons which might prove hard to hold back as they hurtled down from the hump.

The fundamental progress through the Up yard involved the engine of an arriving train being released to March Loco via the engine road and a shunter uncoupling between wagons for each onward destination. A 'Cut Card' showing the number and broad weight type of each separation was compiled, then passed to the control tower to become the basis for setting the 'King' and 'Queen' points which controlled the onward access to the various sorting sidings, and for the degree of restraint pressure applied by the retarder operators. The Class 08 diesel would then propel each train of separated wagon cuts up and over the raised hump at a steady 1.5mph, with the descent slope separating the cuts sufficiently for the point and retarder operations carried out in the control tower. 'Wagon chasers' in the reception sidings would apply brakes on individual wagons if they were running too fast, with a pilot engine doing a bit of 'pushing down' if not fast enough.

In due course the newly made-up 'trains' were drawn on to the departure sidings, a brake van was dropped on by gravity from the 'brake kip' and, with the engine from March Loco backing onto the front, they could go on their way once they 'got the road'.

Of course, there was so much more to it than this – a defective wagon to be examined and shunted out, another 'off the road' and needing re-railing, an incoming engine 'on its knees' or men not 'knowing the road' for their next working. In Norwood, getting the pick-up fruit trains in on time in the season and transferring their vans to the waiting night-fitted freights was a masterly and hectic performance in its own right.

All this mixture, a traffic apprentice was supposed to see and understand. In the odd quiet corner he had to master the use of a shunting pole, and he was expected to work all three shifts – out in the pouring rain in the middle of the night on many occasions, but then learning just how good a cup of tea in a warm mess hut could taste. He took shifts in each of the numerous signal boxes and had the less glamorous, but somewhat more comfortable, task of spending time in the offices getting to grips with all the staff and traffic records that such a complex operation inevitably entailed.

This was one of the 'sharp ends' of railway activity, quite tough but immensely interesting.

STATIONS AND YARDS

Shades of Brunel

Interspersed between my periods of training at Whitemoor and then at March Motive Power Depot was one directed towards increasing my understanding of front-line passenger and freight traffic operation. It was highly varied and valuable with the added dividend of allowing me one or two extra nights at home. Ian was now nearly 7 and at a local Enfield school, and his brother nearing 2, both pretty lively and a major responsibility for Sheila. Home ownership also brought its expenses and labours, but we had

Ivatt Large Atlantic 4-4-0 No 4441 at the head of an Up Cambridge Buffet Express, just one example of the wide variety of motive power formerly to be seen at Cambridge.

built up a circle of friends and money was not quite as tight as in the past. On one visit to my folks at Norwich I had even splashed out on a fur coat for my wife, as some small recognition for the burden she was carrying.

This period began with some time at Cambridge, a place I knew well from our earlier days nearby in Bedfordshire and journeys to and from Norwich and my RAF base at Marham. Now I was able to get behind the scenes and derive some real understanding of this rather complicated meeting point of four former railway companies – the Great Northern Railway, the Great Eastern Railway, the London and North Western Railway (LNWR), and the Midland Railway (MR) – and its complex of a long four-direction-working platform and three bays, plus eight assorted freight yards. From the south end and under the control of the South signal box, services departed for Colchester, Liverpool Street, King's Cross and Bedford/Bletchley, and at the other end the North box managed the trains to Ipswich, Norwich, King's Lynn/Hunstanton and via March/Peterborough and Kettering as well as those on the Mildenhall branch and via St Ives.

Despite a great deal of railway travel and experience, I have never since come across a place that equalled Cambridge in operational awkwardness. It reminded me of Brunel's ideas on station platform layout. The central double crossover in the main lines, which enabled access to the two ends of the long single platform, meant a high level of conflicting movements, as did the way the freight yards were scattered on either side of those two main lines. It was a great place for train spotters, with engine types ranging from the ubiquitous 2-4-0 E4 Class machines that worked the Colchester route trains to a host of GER 'Clauds', B1s, B12s and B17s on the more important workings. Midland types came in from the Kettering route, LNWR designs from Bedford and more variety from the Hitchin direction. The newer British Railways (BR) standard classes were appearing, as were diesel multiple units and even railbuses. This was a mixture calculated to cause problems for the locomotive superintendent, Geoff Parslew, and his shedmaster, who also had to be ready for the occasional Royal Train movements to Sandringham. A spotless relief engine had to be on standby on such occasions.

A Badge of Authority

In contrast, my next station was a much simpler affair. March's four main platforms dealt with some important trains from Cambridge, Ipswich and Norwich for GN&GE joint-line destinations and others on to Peterborough East and beyond. There were three west end bays for trains to King's Lynn and others, and a goods avoiding line to help with keeping the Whitemoor services away from those carrying passengers. The level crossing bottleneck at the London end was a major problem, but extra Up and Down goods lines eastwards and some permissive and wrong direction working authorities kept the traffic moving, except at peak holiday times when the three signal boxes had their hands full with extra services and a lot of engine changes.

District Inspector Percy Baynes had an office on Platform 1 at March and, being a great guy, gave me free access to it and to his advice and guidance. But one morning I was greeted with: 'Young man, your appearance is just not acceptable.'

Discomforted, I muttered, 'Why on earth not; what's wrong with my suit and nondescript coat?'

'People are just not sure who you are,' replied Percy, 'so they treat you with suspicion and you don't get the best out of them.'

At this, like a stage magician, he produced a spare district inspector's mackintosh, needing a little patching, but entirely venerable and vesting its wearer with that feeling of being on the inside that was always accorded to inspectors and the like. It was to serve me well.

After the sessions at Cambridge and March, plus an odd day at Broxbourne, I had a period back in Whitemoor General Offices and then one in the Traffic Costing Office at the ER Liverpool Street headquarters. The effort to understand its true costs and allocate them by activity was an important feature of the changing railway, but I could not find in it the degree of satisfaction I was getting from my widening operational experience.

A Real Mixture of Yards

This was now to be extended by visits to four more freight yards, at Colwick, Pyewipe, New England and Norwich. And so it was that on 23 May, I clambered up into the brake van of the 9.10 a.m. goods train to Colwick and introduced myself to the guard. We were equally astonished to find that we had the same surname, but no relatives in common. I had two days to explore and understand this important yard, which lay where the Grantham, Nottingham and Annesley lines formed a triangle. The main traffics sorted were Northamptonshire iron ore and coal from the local collieries, plus the usual mix of general goods, empties and so on. All the sorting in its forty-odd sidings was of the basic sort, steam pilots, basic points' frames and directions by hand, lamp, voice or whistle code. It was all very antiquated by today's standards, but a marvellous demonstration of traditional shunting skills.

Pyewipe, situated just north of Lincoln Central, where the Lancashire, Derbyshire and East Coast Railway (LDECR) line west to Tuxford makes junction with the Retford/Gainsborough route, was smaller, simpler and less impressive, just a mix of four small siding groups and a lot of coal traffic sorting. New England, in contrast, was quite confusing and very difficult to work, not least because, being located on the Up side of the East Coast main line just north of the Peterborough North station and with a bottleneck at each end, there was great difficulty in getting trains on and off the main line. I noted that all the yards were flat apart from one with a small knuckle, and recorded: 'Yards are a conglomeration of haphazard sidings with so much inter-yard transfer that one pilot is occupied full time thereon.'

The Norwich yards were different, but not much less awkward to work. There were fourteen locations altogether, made more complicated to service by being grouped before and beyond the old Trowse station and the swing bridge crossing of the River Wensum which follows. The former Eastern Union terminus at Norwich Victoria was still dealing with freight at that time and had to send its pilot down to fetch traffic ex Whitemoor from the sidings near the junction of the two London routes. When more than twenty wagons were involved, the train engine would stay on at one end with the pilot at the other to cope with the rise as the Ipswich line climbs to cross the one to Ely.

MOTIVE POWER 🏴

On the Inside – of a Firebox!

I suppose there had been a time when, like so many lads of that era, I would have thought that spending four weeks in a major railway locomotive depot was the ultimate in satisfaction. In fact, such places were hectic, dirty and confusing, but even so, they had a very special atmosphere that no other part of the railway could provide. It derived superficially from the sheer presence of the machines themselves but, more meaningfully, from the essential truth that they energised all railway activity.

Situated on the south side of Whitemoor Yard, the March Loco lines and plant associated with the basic engine running – washout shed, coal plant, sand plant, inspection tunnel, turntable, ash plant, etc. – were grouped parallel with the marshalling yard's Down group of sidings, with the engine shed and workshops sited between there and the Peterborough line.

A typical freight locomotive line-up at March Motive Power Depot, in this case with J15 Class No 65474 sandwiched between two 'Austerity' 2-8-0s.

The former area was controlled by the running foreman with an outside foreman and an ashpit foreman to assist him.

The basic locomotive establishment when I began my training period at March Motive Power Depot was of 143 machines to work 97 diagrams. On a typical day, March would engine around 140 trains, 90-odd of which would be its own diagrams. Of the 140, about 20 would be passenger turns, slightly fewer would be express freights and the others unfitted freight workings. The staff establishment was around 1,100 people, 35 per cent of whom were shed and workshop staff and most of the remainder footplate staff. In common with other depots, the latter were organised on a 'link' basis with No 1 Junior Spare Fireman link leading in stages to No. 4 Main Line Spare, then rising through the seniority levels to No. 9 Express Passenger and then down with age through locals, shunting and eventually shed turning.

I had been received kindly by shedmaster Harry Webster and then handed over to his running foreman for the first few days. A dose of reality followed when I was passed to the ashpit foreman and under his direction made acquaintance with the whole down-to-earth process of locomotive examination, washout and testing the condition of the firebox – from inside!

On to the boilersmith and I was put to another of the good-natured tests that practical working railwaymen were in the habit of presenting to traffic apprentices, that of building a brick arch. All this I survived and learned from and the week was rounded off by an outing with the breakdown van to re-rail a bogie bolster wagon on the Up hump in Whitemoor yard. Their length and heavy loads meant such wagons were always a bit of a risk and I remember marvelling at one incident where a following wagon on the descent to the sorting sidings partially knocked a Bobol from under its load of steel bars, only to have yet another wagon knock it back into position. No one but myself was the wiser.

Tapping and Shopping

A week with the mechanical foreman followed, absorbing the whole mechanics of distance-based locomotive maintenance, repair and shopping. There was time at the wheeldrop and an invitation to emulate the wheel tapping that I had so often witnessed before as an ordinary train traveller. Given a hammer and examples of a sound wheel and a cracked one, I could at least tell the difference. Especially interesting was the re-railing of locomotive 63803 using the German Kelbus gear, essentially a series of pulleys to translate the normal assisting engine tow into one much slower and more controllable. Ahead lay a week of travelling on the footplate. Practical though I was trying to be, I was excited at the prospect.

By this stage I had a pretty good understanding of the motive power function and procedures and, from my earlier weeks, of the tasks to be performed. In addition to recognising the importance of engine availability figures, the proportion of productive time in rosters, costs of coaling and a host of other such crucial indicators, I was beginning to sense some of the underlying layers of difficulty and challenge. For example, the March locomotive stock comprised no fewer than thirteen different steam locomotive types, with the numbers of each ranging from one Class 9F to twenty-five K1s and a similar number of O1s. There were forty 0-6-0s, twelve 4-6-0 B17s and six 2-6-2 V1s for the passenger jobs and ten diesel-electrics. In daily practice, though, actual availability made it very difficult to allocate the right type of machine to individual diagrams.

On the Footplate

This complex basic situation was reflected on the footplate. For prestigious trains on the East Coast main line, a footplate crew would get a familiar locomotive. Not so at March, with the result that drivers and firemen had to develop the skills of getting the best from whatever machine they got and apply them effectively to whatever job was required. On my first day, Driver Wakeling and Fireman Burgess were fortunate to get B17 4-6-0 *Champion Lodge* when they booked on at 1.43 p.m. to take over a Newcastle–Lowestoft passenger train booked to leave March at 2.03 p.m. The engine was handed over in good trim, some enthusiastic firing gave us plenty of steam for our easily-graded run, and we ran into Norwich Thorpe station a few minutes ahead of time. After staying with the crew while the coaling, watering and turning were carried out, I took the opportunity to nip up to take a quick tea with my parents before getting back to the loco to return on the 7.38 p.m. Class D freight, which we got to Whitemoor's Down reception sidings promptly at 10.19 p.m.

This first easy day was followed by a much more tiring one. Booking on at 9.54 a.m. for Diagram No 19 produced another B17, this time No. 61619 *Welbeck Abbey,* to work the 10.34 Parkeston Quay to Liverpool service between March and Sheffield. With the rear driving wheels tucked close under the footplate, B17s were noted for their rough riding and the potential for the lap plate between engine and tender to produce a sawing motion which would have the boot heels off the unwary.

To make matters worse, 61619 was fresh out of shops and very 'stiff in the bushes' – something that would wear off, but not during our trip. We had a heavy load both outwards and back with the 2.59 p.m. return working and, despite the valiant efforts of Driver Ward and Fireman Ellington, we lost time both ways.

In contrast to my experience with *Welbeck Abbey,* the next day's allocation of Class V2 No 60803 was a delight. Long my favourite locomotive type for looks, performance and utility, the V2 handled the morning March to York portion of the Lowestoft–Newcastle service like a dream. Getting away at 40 per cent cut off and then gently notching up, Driver Head was off north to a smooth start that was to be a feature of his handling for the whole journey. Fireman Robinson seemed to make light work of coaling a good fire and attending to the injectors so that, as we sped up the joint line, I was given the chance to take over the care of the fire.

'Put the coal where the fire is burning brightest,' advised Fireman Robinson, and then studiously and thoughtfully ignored me, so as not to cause too much embarrassment as I tried to follow his advice and emulate his skills.

More thoughtfulness as, after a while, he enquired, 'How are you getting on?'

Some rush of honesty compelled me to reply, 'I reckon if I can keep my footing and get the coal through that ridiculously small firebox door I've done well, never mind where it goes when it gets inside there!' Fortunately this was taken in good part and received with a good-humoured smile.

A Lucky Escape

At Retford, quite unwittingly, I could have caused a serious problem when I got down to the platform to stretch my legs for a moment and responded in the affirmative to my driver's enquiry, 'All right, mate?'

I said yes, but what I took to be an enquiry after my well-being was actually one about the readiness of the train to depart. Fortunately, no one was caught half in and half out of the coaches. Driver Head came from Norfolk and in the mess room at York, while we waited for the 2.50 p.m. return, I witnessed the interesting spectacle of him in conversation with a real Geordie driver, an exchange full of rich dialect and occasional misunderstandings.

The pattern of good day–bad day continued on the morrow when we lumbered up the joint line with an unfitted goods train and Class 01 No. 63875. Driver Bradman and Fireman Southwell got us to Pywipe without notable incident at 10.52 a.m., but instead of working back with 63875 on our booked diagram, we were given K3 No 61887 to bring a Class C fitted train back. Our new engine rode like a pig, steamed badly, made a lot of ominous noises and wasted water recklessly. It took all the crew's experience and skill to get us back without the train being 'dyked' or causing too much delay.

My final footplate day was an easy one with a Class H Whitemoor–Bury St Edmunds working one way and a Class D partially-fitted goods the other. I had formed a poor opinion of B1 4-6-0s from commuting into King's Cross, but they were not designed for suburban train work and, despite injector trouble, our B1, No 61360, made light work of the run to Bury. We had No 61252 for the return journey and she had a hot big end, but Driver Bird and Fireman Lacey still got us home on time. Back in the yard reception sidings at 3.25 p.m., since it was a Friday I took advantage of the early return and headed homewards. It had been an incredible week, full of valuable and impressive experiences.

A Unique Tramway

Before moving on to the final parts of my motive power training, I had a trip out to Wisbech and then on the roadside tramway to Upwell. Although coal was still being delivered to the depots along the route of the former Wisbech Canal, returning with fruit in season, the once busy days on this unique line had passed and road transport was now taking that portion of the crops which could be picked later and still reach the markets in good time. The line was worked by two 204hp diesels booked to make return trips with passenger-rated traffic at 4 p.m. and freight-rated consignments at 5 p.m. Re-engined at Wisbech, the vans were then conveyed to the Norwood Yard at Whitemoor, which shunted seven of the more urgent inwards loadings from the whole fruit-growing area between 5.38 p.m. and 6.33 p.m., and another four second-priority trains between 7.22 p.m. and 8.15 p.m. This was shunting at its most intense, ensuring connections were made with the evening express freight trains to the London and the northern provincial markets.

I am so glad I had the opportunity to see lines like this Wisbech & Upwell Tramway, the Wissington Light Railway, the Mid-Suffolk, and branches like those to Benwick and Eye. Even the best efforts of today's heritage railways could not adequately recreate a period Wisbech & Upwell train with its faired-in, tram-like locomotive, peculiar coaches, rake of vans and the mobile office behind – all performing a useful service to the community.

Diesel and Electric

The move on to Norwich Diesel Depot meant leaving my lodgings at March and saying farewell to the Brands. I was quite sorry to go, for they had made me very welcome and comfortable. But my schedule called and the first day at Norwich began with a diesel multiple unit cab trip to Lowestoft and back, reviving memories of the journeys I had made over the same route during the East Anglian herring season over a decade earlier. The depot itself had Metro Cammell and Derby units to look after and, despite my short time there, I managed to acquire some basic knowledge of the engineering issues as well as the problems of vibration, coupling incompatibilities and other such matters.

The next stop was the Electric Traction Depot at Ilford, home to ninety-two 3-car sliding door train sets for the eighty-four GE main-line diagrams and thirty-two 4-car sets for twenty-nine Southend diagrams. Too little examination space and some peculiar rostering were causing utilisation problems, but a new shed was then in the course of construction and would remedy those issues. Power for these train operations was controlled from the Chadwell Heath Electrical Control Room, whose staff were tasked with overseeing the intake power supplies from the grid and the onwards distribution to sub-stations where it was rectified to the 1,500-volt direct current used by the electric trains. This was another very informative time for me and was followed by cab trips to Chelmsford and Southend to see how it all worked out in practice.

The end of my motive power training was now approaching. I still had a session at the Ilford depot, which undertook the cleaning of the electric units and the provision of motormen from the establishment of 102 such posts. Finally, a few days in the headquarters Utilisation Section brought all the various strands of the previous few weeks together under staff dealing with maintenance, staffing, new works, engine allocations, irregularities, accidents and delays, special trains and so on. The section's inspectors dealt with signal sighting, trials and the instruction in the diesel school.

CAMBRIDGE: COMMERCIAL AND OPERATING 🖙

Views from the Garret

On 15 July 1957, I reported to the Cambridge offices and received a positive welcome. After being in the front line of railway activity for the past few months and learning such a lot in the process, I felt that going back to passive instruction in the offices of the Cambridge District commercial manager would be something of an anticlimax, especially as I already had some experience in this area from my Gordon Hill days. The reality turned out to be very different, for despite the country nature of the territory, the district office dealt with some quite substantial and varied movements of goods and people. The freight movements, which I studied first, included those of two British Sugar Corporation factories, tanks and other items from the army and air force bases, a huge amount of frozen and tinned food produce from around King's Lynn and some specialised items like caravans and the Newmarket race traffic, people and horses.

Getting somewhere to lodge was the first priority and local recommendation sent me to see an old couple who had a garret I could have; they seemed quite pleased with the prospect of both my company and my contribution to their income. The latter proved just a little more than we had discussed, for when each evening meal had been cleared away they would bring out the playing cards and give me costly lessons in playing rummy.

Starting my office tour in the Cartage & Terminals Section, familiar territory for me, I was able to accompany Inspector Robinson when he paid a visit to Ely and Wisbech. Interestingly, the former regularly helped Cambridge out with its periodical surge of university luggage by sorting it into cartage areas. Both the Wisbech stations, North and East, had tramway connections to the harbour, with small ships discharging timber direct to wagon, for it then to be moved by shunting tractor for BR staff to sheet and rope prior to the main journey. Both stations were also exceptionally busy in the Cambridgeshire fruit season, and if a ship arrived at the same time, life could get a little hectic.

At this stage I was able to grab a week off and we took a rather unadventurous family holiday at Clacton, where sitting in a deckchair in the sun or taking tea in our rented beach hut proved just what Sheila and I needed. We met the Storrie family, a lovely older couple from Colchester whose vivacious daughter Brenda seemed happy to keep our boys amused while we recuperated.

After an interesting period absorbing the diversity and complexities of the Cambridge Rates & Charges Section and the Claims Section, I was back on the ground at Saffron Walden helping to search for missing wagons and to check that rolling stock, sheets, ropes, etc. were all being used efficiently and not just left lying around. Then it was on to RAF Marham to measure a vehicle to be despatched by rail, quite a nostalgic occasion as I had spent much of my National Service there.

Another outdoor visit was to King's Lynn, where three main rail routes converged before heading on to the terminal station and the line on to the sea at Hunstanton, and to the connections for the riverside wharves and the enclosed docks. The river quays were Corporation owned and operated, with vessels of up to 3,000 tons bringing in phosphates for the Norfolk Farmers Manure Company, and the Alexander and Bentinck docks, run by the Docks & Inland Waterways Executive, were providing us with a substantial amount of timber traffic.

With the claims enquiry clerk, I paid another visit to King's Lynn to look into an alleged shortage in a consignment sent to Travis & Arnold at Cambridge. All sorts of difficulties came to light, for the timber was very difficult to tally and recording tended to take second place to vessel turnround. The next day took us to Wisbech because of problems there with tinplate for the Metal Box Company. The slightest damage to the inwards sheet tin caused difficulty in feeding it into the firm's machines, while outwards mechanised loading of the finished tins was prone to transit 'jumbling'.

More office studies, including the large potential of livestock and the considerable passenger traffic, brought me to the end of my time in the commercial offices. To mark this I was given the specific task of reporting on whether the small stations of Linton and Pampisford should be reduced in status to unstaffed halts and public delivery sidings with the forthcoming dieselisation of the Haverhill line. I spent a couple of October days extracting details of the passenger and freight activity at those places which, to everyone's surprise, turned out to be more than thought, enough to allow me to recommend no reduction in status.

A prelude to moving from the Cambridge commercial activity to that of the district operating people had been my deployment on a passenger survey on the East Coast main line, starting on the Monday with the 9 a.m. from King's Cross to Darlington and back with the 2.14 p.m., quite a taxing day handing out questionnaires and then discussing the answers with those who responded. I could only croak when I got in that evening, but learned to pace myself later. The response to one questionnaire made it clear that the couple alone in the compartment with all the blinds drawn down had been continuing their honeymoon and didn't mind who knew it!

On another occasion my opposite number travelling on an Up train from Scotland had moved some second-class passengers into a First Open coach, doubtless for some good reason. When I joined and took over, it was to find that the travelling ticket collector had obliged them to pay the fare difference and some diplomacy was needed to sort the confrontation out.

By the end of the survey week I was exhausted and seemed to be nurturing a cold. After finishing the subsequent job of analysing the results at Liverpool Street headquarter offices, I joined my wife in succumbing to Asian flu and retired to my bed to recover.

Signals and Perks

My first day with the Cambridge operating staff proved memorable for all the wrong reasons. Out with the bluff Yorkshireman, District Inspector Epton, we had a good look round Bury St Edmunds and then returned to Newmarket for what proved to be a liquid lunch. Foolishly, I tried to keep pace in the art of ale consumption and began to pay the penalty as soon as we parted company. Somehow I got back to the station by carefully walking along the shadow of some fencing, joined the right train by instinct, spent most of the journey in the toilet and, back at Cambridge, collapsed in a woozy sleep on a waiting room bench seat. It was mid-evening by the time I woke, still feeling decidedly unwell but thankful that no one seemed to have seen me in my decidedly un-management-like condition.

Rejoining DI Epton for some exploration of the two cross-country routes from Cambridge towards Colchester, I had resolved to steer clear of lunchtime alcohol and concentrate on the intricacies of single-line signalling. I understood the basic principles of using a staff or token to denote the right to traverse a single line, but there seemed to be a large number of refinements to grasp. At Glemsford, for example, all passenger trains used the single platform, leaving the passing loop for goods train shunting. The signal box had been retained as a ground frame to control the points for the second line and the section tablet was needed to gain access to it. In the case of an Up train from Long Melford to Sudbury, the porter there collected the token from the driver, checked that the train was complete with tail lamp and clear of the entry to the loop, advised the signalman of this by telephone and then inserted the collected token into his own auxiliary instrument. The signalman could then take a token from his auxiliary instrument in the box, place it in the main one and send the 'Train Out of Section' bell signal back to Long Melford.

A further complication was that the token instruments were not all standardised. As a result, an error with a Tyers No 2 instrument could not be corrected and the token had to be taken through the section, sometimes just by bicycle, to put matters right. There was also a special 4-4-4-4 bell code for use by the signal and telegraph staff to adjust the stock of tokens if there had been more movements in one direction than in the other. All this I took in, along with visits to Bury junction box, which controlled access to the line to Thetford, and the BSC factory, for which, again, there were special arrangements.

Over the next week or so, using passenger trains, goods trains, lifts and cycling, I spent some time at all the stations along these two lines and also had a trip out to Felstead and Braintree. DI Epton was on leave the latter part of the time, so I was able to choose my location and, under close supervision by the signalmen, worked the boxes at Clare and Haverhill without causing any incidents. A little bit of self-indulgence during a visit to Long Melford had me walking out to the site of Borley Rectory, which had intrigued me since I first read Harry Price's book *The Most Haunted House in England*. I am not sure what I expected but, as it turned out, there was nothing to see. A last few days of working Kennett signal box, double lines for a change, ended the Epton period and passed me on to District Inspector Herbert Deller.

A Memorable Lunch

With DI Deller I began another round of station and signal box visits, this time along the Hunstanton line, as far as Postland on the joint line and west to the Peterborough East area. These all brought new situations and new learning experiences, interluded with the occasional more relaxing moments like a November walk on the beach at Heacham and the purchase of fish and chips to eat on our returning train. Another return journey was on an experimental fitted coal train. More stressful was a practical session in the box at Magdalen Road on a day of dense fog. Working the frame with no visual sense of the outside situation was quite unnerving, with the Down passenger train due and the pick-up goods train in the yard whistling to be allowed on its way. Not being able to confirm visually that the latter had not moved without authority was quite disturbing, and I was glad that I had people watching my actions.

March-based DI Percy Baynes, who had become a good friend, was my mentor for a visit to Whittlesea and its brickyard sidings. We usually managed a bread and cheese lunch on these visits, with a half of the local brew and a quick game of darts to tone me up for the afternoon's absorption of knowledge. March locomotive depot canteen was also a regular calling point, but one particular lunchtime elsewhere stands out very vividly in my recall.

In this period I had also spent time with Chief Inspector Cyril Rose and his deputy Stan Simpson, going with them to places like Audley End, Coldham depot and Shippea Hill. By the time of our visit to Shippea Hill we were into December, when Fenland looks at its least attractive. Furthermore, the isolated station pub there was a very ordinary-looking place, and when my tuition in the equally ordinary bar stretched as far as 2 p.m. without any sign of anything more than the usual half pint, I resigned myself to this being a day devoid of any lunch. Then a door leading off the bar opened and a lady called dramatically, 'It's ready.'

I followed Cyril and Stan into the back room and was astounded at what I saw. Centrepiece was a table laid out with as fine a display of linen and tableware as I had seen in the Great Eastern Hotel. And this was to be matched by a meal that was equally up to that standard. I think my mentors enjoyed my astonishment and I realised more fully that, despite having to tackle many difficult situations and difficult conditions, the DIs – members of 'The Cloth' as they were known because of their long black macs – knew how to look after their creature comforts when the job allowed.

I was also involved in a study of boundaries, graphing for the revision of Whittlesea train services and attending an accident enquiry. There was a lot of reading to be done and the onerous task of writing careful reports for the local officers and the TA Committee. With the energy of youth I was still preaching as a Methodist lay preacher in the Enfield area at weekends and building a fitted kitchen in our Enfield home, though not nearly fast enough for my wife's liking. Not that I would complain about her urgings, for she was carrying the considerable burden of keeping home and family functioning during my absences. Despite our son Richard contracting chickenpox, our Christmas break proved very welcome before the launching on my second year of training.

The last outside visits before moving into a period in the offices included Godmanchester to experience Direction/Acceptance Lever working, and Ely, which controlled the electric token movements on the Soham line and the staff protection on the Sutton line. After going out to Mildenhall in the brake van of a Class K goods train, I could put aside my heavier outdoor clothing and take in the mysteries of, firstly, the operating function's Works, Accident & General section.

More Variety

It would be tedious to go through the great range of things covered by the staff of this section, but the duties of one post, just Class III grade, might help to convey a sense of the variety that was managed:

> machinery records and cleaning of water tanks
> examination of fire devils and detonators
> station cycles, clocks and lamps
> sale of condemned sheets and stores
> engine mileage records
> weighing machines
> turntable repair and examination
> water column repairs

shopping of engines
experimental engine fittings
hire of steam cranes
safety valves
six-monthly depot inspections
wheel, tyre and axle returns
depot repairs
water treatment
boiler inspections.

Other activities were equally complex, not least the control of level crossings. At this time there were still hundreds of crossings with the traditional hand-operated gates presided over by a crossing keeper. Many were very remote and the job was not very well paid, but the accommodation, though tiny, was the lure that kept them staffed and the wife of a local porter or lengthman could help to supplement the family income by taking on the crossing keeper's job. At one rural level crossing a Polish countess was the incumbent, but she, sadly, was injured when a train ran through the gates. Another lady crossing keeper had her washing on the line when the ballast cleaning train was passing and her language on finding it covered in ballast dust became legendary.

My period in this section had been interrupted twice, first by a week of participation in a punctuality drive which I spent at Broxbourne, trying to cut station delays and recording results, and then travelling on *The Fenman* from Newmarket to test passenger reactions to new prototype coaches built by the Birmingham Carriage & Wagon employees. Unfortunately, this latter exercise collapsed midweek due to troubles with the vehicle lighting.

As the following days and weeks passed, still losing small sums each evening when not working to the elderly Coopers in my digs, I moved on to the Staff Section and then to Passenger Movements, there to get immersed in such different things as schemes for the introduction of diesel multiple units (DMUs) and railbuses and the arrangements for royal and VIP travel. In the Freight Movements Section it was subjects like the complications attending engineers' line possessions, trial trains and also the inevitable mass of statistics relating to every activity.

At the beginning of March, the Monday of my week allocated to the Control Office was actually devoted to participating at Ely in a study of how rust which had accumulated on the wheels of wagons that had been in storage affected the operation of track circuits when they were put back into use.

Then I was shadowing the deputy chief controller (DCC), absorbing the elements of his main task of overseeing and reporting on train running performance. He also managed the allocation of unused train paths for helping to ease congestion and heavy traffic concentrations, this entailing liaison with Regional Control and other districts. The DCC supervised five control 'tables', one each for the areas north and south of Cambridge and others for Whitemoor–Peterborough, the ex-LMS lines and the M&GN joint lines. There was also a controller responsible for enginemen and one for guards, plus a man handling all the statistics of delays, utilisation, shortages and the like.

There was no emergency while I was in the Control Office, but the arrangements for reacting to major difficulties I saw to be impressive: links with the police and other emergency services, information on flood alerts and its dissemination, weather forecasts from the RAF and drawing additional labour from the district engineer, the Ministry of Labour or HM Forces – all part of a response machinery with a very sound base and high capability.

THE FINAL PHASE 🖅

Off to the Seaside
From mid-March to mid-May I was in the headquarter offices of the Great Eastern line traffic manager, gaining an understanding of how all that I had seen and heard fitted together and why.

On the Movements side, for example, there were sections dealing with Passenger Movements, Freight Movements, Terminals & Cartage, Timing and Diagramming and also the Line Control Office. In addition to the day-to-day issues, it was in this period that I obtained a glimpse of the future, including the increasing concentration of freight traffic on fast services between major distribution centres and the carriage of coal in full trainloads to mechanised unloading depots. Forty people were engaged in the complex business of timing and diagramming services.

I moved on to the Commercial group, and then those for Motive Power, Signalling, Works, Staff and Public Relations. Traffic Costing, Traffic Accounting and the two rates sections – Freight and Passenger – were the last

Clacton-on-Sea station master Dick Dennis and his summer season assistant, Geoff Body, confer with the signal box on the local telephone circuit.

ports of call before I emerged from this period of largely passive learning to the final training stage, in which I would be placed in specific supplementary working roles which would be used to establish whether I was able to begin repaying the investment that had been made in me. I awaited news of my first placement with a mixture of eagerness and apprehension.

I was not kept in suspense for long. I was to report to Station Master Dick Dennis at Clacton-on-Sea on 2 June and to be the assistant station master there for the busy summer season. This was good and I quickly decided that I would not relinquish the pleasures of home living I had managed while in the HQ offices but, instead, take my family with me. And so it was that we found accommodation with a Mrs Allen, renewed our acquaintance with our Colchester friends, the Storries, and rented a beach hut at Holland-on-Sea so that Sheila and the boys could enjoy a well-deserved summer break. It also became a refuge for me during some pretty hectic days ahead.

My new boss seemed somewhat reserved at first, but no doubt he was weighing up just what sort of help he could expect. That help was not really needed on weekdays, but Saturdays were a different matter. Things went mad from around 7 a.m. onwards with huge numbers of holidaymakers arriving with their multiple children, luggage and enquiries. Many were heading for the huge Butlin's holiday camp at Jaywick and were easily directed to the coaches that would convey them there, but the return a week later was a less straightforward matter. Despite sending someone down to the camp during the week to arrange advance ticket sales, seat reservations and the collection of luggage, the queue outside the station would be long and would last all day.

From Monday to Friday I participated in the normal station management, manning, signal box visits, equipment control, carriage cleaning, checking office practices and so on, but the big task was that of preparing for the Saturday onslaught. To give us the best chance of keeping the activity deluge under control we needed a full plan for every aspect of every train arriving and departing, especially where the incoming locomotive, stock and men were supposed to go next, so that we could make sure they did so. I'd had a bit of a battle getting a uniform hat with the 'Assistant Station Master' legend on it, but I knew this would be vital to identifying myself, especially to incoming enginemen and guards.

And so the first Saturday arrived. Station Master Dennis, myself and the station inspector were out on the platform soon after 6 a.m., making last-minute checks of things like the availability of luggage barrows and water bowsers. Would the first train – one from the Midlands – arrive on time? It was always a good omen if it did. Then it was a case of halting the engine so as not to foul the release points, checking that the footplate men knew their next working and telling them where they could take their break. Hopefully they would be able to confirm the absence of problems with their engine, that they 'knew the road' for their next working and so on. The same sort of check was taking place with the guard, all the time dealing with passenger enquiries, checking the coaches for damage or items left behind, and finally either seeing them off to the carriage sidings for basic cleaning or doing what could be done *in situ* if the turnaround time was short.

Around mid-morning we could confidently expect our first problem, an incoming train running late, a locomotive that was going to be failed or one of our own guards not reporting for duty. That is when some quick thinking was called for, often in the form of 'robbing Peter to pay Paul'. Control would help if they could, and we always kept them in the picture, but much was down to sheer resourcefulness. With the new Brush diesels now appearing and footplate staff still getting used to them, we could expect the occasional failure, while sometimes there would be a serious passenger incident, anything from drunkenness to fisticuffs to serious illness. Despite all the complications, we survived, but the memory of staggering home in a state of sheer exhaustion every Saturday is still with me.

And thus my three months at Clacton passed, with the Saturday melee easing as the summer drew to a close. There had, of course, been other events of special interest, like the launch of the prestige Essex Coast Express and a Progress Chaser scheme that encouraged youngsters to travel and record and report on what they noted of the advancing electrification works. We had a coach derailment while Dick Dennis was on leave and I was in charge, and my first instinct was to call out the Stratford crane. Reflection and better advice prevailed and the experts in the breakdown van had the vehicle back on the rails with a much less dramatic use of their ramps.

The Other Extreme

A complete change was now to follow, from passenger traffic matters to freight, seaside to the Hackney Marshes and summer to winter. From 15 September I took up the post of supernumerary assistant to the yard master at Temple Mills. Located to the north of the huge Stratford railway activity complex, on what had once been lonely marshes, a modern marshalling yard there had replaced an out-of-date one and taken over the work of several East London yards, including Goodmayes and Thames Wharf.

The new ER marshalling yard at Temple Mills, Stratford, replaced a motley collection of old yards there, along with several others in the East London area.

I duly reported to Yard Master Dan Rose, a terrier of a man who ruled his new empire as he had the previous one, in an energetic and semi-tyrannical way. His wartime exploits in keeping traffic moving during the worst of the 1940s bombing were legendary. Typical of my new boss's methods was to telephone the signal box nearest to the hump to ask if the hump shunting signal was off. If not, there was another call, this time to the hump cabin and with the sharp, accusatory, 'Why aren't you shunting?'

Dan had little patience with anything but shunting wagons effectively, certainly disdaining systems, statistics, paperwork in general and specifically requests from above for information. I thus slipped easily into the role of providing the new yard with a workable backing administration. When Dan retired (not all that willingly, I suspect), he was replaced by my old Whitemoor boss Harry Onyon, whose calm experience was just what was needed. He was happy for me to continue in the previous role but, that organised, I could now make a bigger contribution to the outside activity. For example, by travelling each morning from Enfield to Silver Street and changing there to a Palace Gates–North Woolwich train, I could alight at Lea Bridge and walk through the yard to the office, taking due note of the traffic situation on the way and thus being able to report it to the morning conference when I arrived.

Getting the staff records and other such matters organised took up quite a bit of my time, but it introduced me to practical personnel management on a sizeable scale. Eventually this was all sorted, including the whole range of Local Departmental Committee meetings and negotiations with the trade unions. I was then free to take on more troubleshooting in the yard and such special tasks as running the Sunday testing programme for the new retarders. Another matter I became involved in was the closure of the former guards' dormitory, which was no longer needed under the revised train pattern. In a severe building at the south end of the yard, the dormitory gave the impression of a slightly improved Victorian workhouse, rows of iron bedsteads, simple lockers and basic washing and toilet areas. Our inventory revealed a stock of twenty-nine Victorian chamber pots, which Harry suggested I might like to have at a knock-down price in the hope that they might eventually have a value as collectors' items. What Sheila would have said had I accepted the offer, I hate to think.

I was already being used by Ken Dixon, the Liverpool Street freight assistant, to report on special aspects of the yard working. He was not happy about some previous recommendations to alter certain train and engine movements, and I still have a copy of the report in which the yard master and I strongly opposed them. After eight months in this very interesting post, fellow trainee Geoff Herbert was sent to replace me and I was transferred to the Liverpool Street offices and did a number of other special studies for both Ken Dixon and Chief Controller David Cobbett. These special tasks included revision of the Freight Train Loads Book and a closure study of the Ongar line depots. Three more months there and I began to hear that TAs who had started training in my intake had successfully secured placement in permanent positions. What would be my fate? I was ready and eager to resume my interrupted working career.

THE TRAMWAY

Varied and Profitable

After unsuccessful interviews for the jobs of goods agent at Boston and sales assistant at Ipswich came a very tough interview for the Special Category B Head of Sales & Development Section in the Line Traffic Manager's

Clearly still deep in the paper age, Geoff Body sits at his desk in the London, Tilbury & Southend (LT&S) line's London headquarters in Saracen's Head House near Fenchurch Street station.

Office (LT&S) at Fenchurch Street. I was successful and on 7 September 1959 began a period of hard, varied and rewarding work which was to last until 25 October 1962. Still living in Enfield, my daily commute was to Liverpool Street and an easy walk through to Saracen's Head House, near Fenchurch Street station. In those days a glance down Whitechapel Road occasionally held the drama of seeing a couple of the seamstresses brawling over something or other. Chinatown was still Chinatown then and I was fascinated by the variety that was East London, the remaining slums, the diverse population, the trading tradition and, especially, the buoyant spirit.

J.W. Dedman (JWD) was the line traffic manager, Ted Taylor his commercial assistant and Geoff Foulger the senior sales assistant. Other senior staff include Bob Arnott and Jim Urqhart on the operating side, Ron Eccles as the staff assistant and Percy Gillett as public relations officer (PRO). My own section staff of nine included Charlie Dicks (my deputy), Fred Rolfe (party traffic), Derek Harris (freight rates), Rex Allison, 'Mac' Mackay, Pat Barratt, Marie Danielle and sales representatives Eddie Thurley and Fred Spence. We handled the passenger fares and facilities, freight rates, budgeting, statistics, etc. for the busy lines from Fenchurch Street to Shoeburyness via Pitsea and via Tilbury, plus the Ockenden and Thames Haven branches and the lines to Poplar Dock. There was heavy freight traffic from the Thameside depots through Ripple Lane yard and the line enjoyed high status and autonomy because of its profitability.

Mine was a baptism of fire. My predecessor, Geoff Foulger, whom I knew from my Norwich days and who had now become one of the line's two management staff sales assistants, introduced me to the senior managers and section chiefs and then to my new office staff. That done, he pointed to the considerable pile of papers on my new desk and remarked casually, 'The line budget needs completing and is already overdue.' He turned to go.

Horrified, I responded, 'You'll guide me, won't you?' – not unreasonably, for I knew little of the territory and even less of its traffics and prospects.

'Sorry, Geoff,' was the blunt reaction. 'I've got my hands full with my own workload. You'll just have to do the best you can.'

So I did, entering figures which owed more to imagination than hard fact, but it passed muster and I could turn to other matters. And these duly arose, thick and fast for the whole of my stay, for the office had a very busy, lively and forceful work ethic. Even at the regular inter-regional meetings I had to attend, I usually took my own work with me so as not to waste precious time. Those hosted by the London Midland Region (LMR) occasionally involved 'lunch' in the Somers Town goods depot staff canteen, something that stays in my mind, not because of the quality of the food but because there was only one teaspoon available and that was anchored to the food counter on a very long chain!

Serviced from the new marshalling yard at Ripple Lane, where Eric Hopwood was yard master, the LT&S line, despite the small size which led its detractors to label it 'The Tramway', had a very considerable freight activity, the main constituents of which will now be described.

Taking Cars off the Road

There was a vast business to and from the Ford Motor Company's Thames-side estate lines and the finished motor car traffic, which we set out to build up through Dagenham Dock. As cars were sold to dealers 'ex works', we had to persuade them to forsake the use of car transporter road vehicles and use our covered carriage trucks (CCTs) and bogie wagons instead, our persuasion being that vehicles would arrive at the showrooms with hardly

The Ford Motor Company's 0-6-0ST No 8 positions the special vans which made up the daily train of motor parts from Dagenham to the Halewood factory.

any mileage on the clock. This task involved Geoff Foulger and me visiting Ford dealers all over the country to get them to put their cars on rail in sufficient numbers to persuade Ford to take over delivery responsibility, a process that eventually raised car carryings from 2,000 in 1958 to some 30,000 in 1962.

My first visit to Ford had produced the courtesy of a guided tour of the main plant areas and with it a rather scary initiation ceremony. The foundry workers were adept at skating red hot metal rods, straight from the furnace and across the floor from one location to another, and made a point of showing their skills by skimming one past each new visitor!

I shall remember my first car sales trip too, down to Plymouth and Launceston. I drove the office Ford Anglia to Paddington for an early train and was able to sit and enjoy a cooked breakfast as the sun shone along the lovely stretch of track down the Exe estuary and along the coast through Dawlish and Teignmouth. Alighting at Plymouth, I asked a porter to keep an eye on my overnight case while I checked something with the local staff. 'Oh sir,' I was rebuked in a rich West Country accent, 'you must be from London. No one down 'ere would touch your things.'

Another journey, this time by road, was to a licensing authority's traffic court at Warwick using the then new M1, quite a novel experience, especially as traffic using it was sparse. This was part of our policy of advancing our own facilities to oppose licence applications from road hauliers for more car transporter vehicles, something I did again later at Leeds and Cockermouth. After our success with carrying cars, another important Ford movement we secured was a daily train of engine parts from Dagenham to Halewood. These trains just had to run to time, for the journey was, to all intents and purposes, part of the Ford production line.

Oil and Water

Another constituent of The Tramway's freight activity was the substantial trainload business of a variety of petrol and oil products in 100-ton tank wagons from the Shell Haven refinery and from Esso's tank farm at Purfleet. As with the other important traffic movements, Geoff Foulger undertook the main negotiations, but I had a face-to-face link with all our major customers and was their main point of contact for quoting rates for new flows and for the subsequent quality of our performance in handling them. Steering a course between the needs of these customers and a somewhat rigid attitude on the part of the headquarters rates people called for some artful manoeuvring on occasions.

The Tramway was also involved in the shipping traffic to and from Tilbury Docks, Poplar Dock South and the Regent's Canal Dock. After my first tour around our dock at Poplar, I became very involved in this small but lucrative business of a working Thameside harbour. Much of the older infrastructure had been rendered derelict by wartime bombing, buildings like the old stables were just a shell, but we had adequate cranage and the quays were in constant use, unloading small vessels and barges.

For cargoes unloaded over the side to barges in the larger Port of London Authority (PLA) docks, we were in fierce competition with the LMR dock at Poplar and the former Great Western Railway (GWR) one at Brentford. I got on well with our agents, Vokins, and we built up a nice little activity in imported wool traffic, frequently stealing a march on the Union Lighterage people who acted for the London Midland.

Another unusual feature in this shipping world was the Guaranteed Tonnage Agreement between BR and the PLA, one inherited by us both and which related to the rail conveyance of imports from Tilbury to East Smithfield. It had been created originally to secure to rail an assured volume of traffic from the furthest downstream dock to a new rail warehouse nearer London, thus making that dock more competitive, and to create the investment for it. The facility had become outmoded and was something the PLA sought desperately to get modified, in order to reduce the shortfall annual payment it was by now having to make.

Social occasions connected with our busy stretch of the River Thames included luncheon on board the SS *City of Ottawa* – I'm not sure what the reason was – and the occasion of the visit of Sir Francis Chichester to the Thames after his amazing round-the-world voyage. Sheila and I watched his triumphant progress upriver from the deck of a tug belonging to the Samuel Williams Estate fleet, the Williams riverside wharves and sidings being used by Ford for moving its vessel imports from shipside to factory.

The Tramway also enjoyed the extensive business arising at Rainham, Purfleet and Grays through the multiple private sidings there. There was packaged timber from the Phoenix Timber Company, the tanker movements from the Purfleet fuel tank farm and bitumen depot, and a good share of the output of the factories of Procter & Gamble, Van den Bergh & Jurgens and Thames Board Mills. There were also negotiations and visits linked to the cement production at Grays, involving CMC/Wouldhams, Tunnel Cement, Lafarge and the Thurrock Chalk & Whiting Company, together handing us a lot of cement traffic in Presflo wagons.

Another riverside firm in this area was the shipbreaking business of T.W. Ward Ltd. I was later to regret not buying some of the lovely brass fittings they could offer at very cheap prices. Former ships' lifeboats were available at that time at £1 per foot of length.

Change and Reward

The LT&S lines also carried a considerable volume of passengers. These included a vast number of commuters using Fenchurch Street station every weekday morning and evening. Coping with this in the period prior to electrification, when the steam locomotives were old and worn out, was a nightmare. The new electric trains and their new maintenance depot at East Ham also brought teething troubles, as did the challenges of devising new fares – for example, within the borough of Southend. Both JWD and I wanted to use the new electric trains to siphon traffic off the Southend buses and argued several times about whether the attraction should be threepence per station travelled or fourpence, but I can't remember which view prevailed.

There was in addition a substantial amount of party business: the St Pancras–Tilbury boat train movements, moving forces baggage to Germany for the British Forces Post Office (BFPO), excursions to Southend for the Illuminations and so on.

The office at Saracen's Head House had a good social side, including an annual dinner at which I had to propose the toast of 'The Ladies' disconcertingly soon after my arrival. Each December we sang carols round a Christmas tree on Fenchurch Street station and, as a member of the Eastern Region Musical Society, I performed in concerts in the London Guildhall, at Sheffield and at other venues. Being in the choir for a rendering of the Easter Hymn in the hallowed surroundings of the Guildhall was a very moving experience.

In contrast, a sad event was a derailment on 18 April 1961 involving the 12.25 p.m. from Fenchurch Street, in which two people were killed and forty-six injured. It occurred at Pitsea where the station master had a reputation as being a bit eccentric. He performed superbly on the occasion of the crash, but had previously had a bit of bother with a bus using the station forecourt as a free overnight parking spot. Payment was refused, so the station master retaliated by chaining the bus to a lamp post.

I had never previously worked quite as hard as I did during this period. My bosses spared neither me nor themselves but were quick to respond with praise or reward when appropriate. My first reward was in September 1961, when I was selected to enjoy the three-day Clyde experience that the Caledonian Steamship Company offered annually to railway staff able to influence passenger business their way. A small group of us were treated like lords, ferried to the Clyde beauty spots and plied with overwhelming hospitality. On my return Commercial Superintendent Ted Taylor, when thanked for the selection, remarked drily that I was the only one who would not be missed! I liked Ted and learned a great deal from him, including a tactic which led him to pass out papers marked for me and annotated, 'You know my views on this.' I admitted once that I often did not and was told, 'I knew that, but also knew it would make you think hard to come up with the most sensible action.'

When Ted Taylor went off to the new Eastern Region headquarters in York, Geoff Foulger got his job. I was summoned to the office of Stan Eccles, our staff man, who had a stern face and looked as if he was about to deliver some bad news. Instead, I was to be promoted to Geoff's former job, jumping a grade to succeed him as MS2 Sales Assistant from 27 August 1962 at a salary of £1,350 p.a., increased to £1,390 under a pay award.

The following July brought the combination of the Fenchurch Street and Liverpool Street offices. For the four months before the two organisations were amalgamated, with Geoff Foulger and Ted Taylor now off to new jobs at York, I was acting Commercial Superintendent LT&S and now on an annual salary of £1,500 – a fair sum for that time. It seemed a far cry from the job of temporary probationary junior male clerk and that first day seventeen years earlier.

I had enjoyed my time on the LT&S, grown in knowledge and ability, and really quite enjoyed the whole process, despite long days and constant hard graft. Not only had my colleagues been a first-class bunch, but the territory, though small, had offered a rich variety in traffic. In the small interludes of non-working time it had also provided the opportunity to discover a lot of social and historic interest, from the surviving traces of the cable-worked London & Blackwall Railway to the French Ordinary Court passage under the Fenchurch Street station approach lines, once the home of the servants of French émigrés and, in my time, of wonderfully scented spice storage.

TRAFFIC MANAGER'S OFFICE AND EASTERN REGION HQ, LIVERPOOL STREET 📠

A Hide on the Docks

Just before the end of the Line Traffic organisation on the Eastern Region (ER), I was detached for a short middle management course from 19–21 June 1963. It was held in a former stately home at Windsor, which was also used to train staff for British Transport Hotels, and they were able to 'practise' on those attending such courses. Today I remember the meals better than the instruction!

From 18 November 1963, the functions of the former LT&S line were embraced in the new organisation of the Traffic Manager, Liverpool Street, which was responsible for all the former Great Eastern Railway (GER) territory in the north-east sector of London, out to Colchester, Clacton, Bishop's Stortford and Hertford. The traffic manager was Harold Few, his commercial manager George Stoddard and I was allocated the MS3 commercial assistant post with a salary rise to £1,745 p.a.

This was the period of electrification of the suburban routes into Liverpool Street and a whole host of teething troubles were encountered, mostly associated with the voltage changeover equipment. I spent a lot of time on staff negotiations, firstly in connection with the Bishopsgate goods depot concentration scheme (which was often argued late into the evening in a Bishopsgate Institute blue with the haze of cigarette smoke) and later ready for the new ER organisation that followed on from the Beeching Report.

I was involved in several significant changes and major activities relating to the freight business, prominent among which was the upheaval resulting from the virtual withdrawal of rail facilities from the inner London docks. However, we were still handling wagon load business through Tilbury, one of the places I had to visit to see if we could improve the loadability of the imported cattle hides which were regularly being forwarded to Moorlands at Glastonbury. To make the business profitable, we had to push the average load up from 9 tons in each wagon at least to 10 tons. With the help of the dock authority and the dock labour we managed it, but not before I had been challenged to experience the loading task for myself. There was no option but to accept – however, moving from unloading point to wagon with a heavy, hot and smelly cow hide over my shoulders and back was not something I would have wanted to do for a living.

Other freight matters in which I was deeply involved included:

the rationalisation of the Silvertown Tramway;
a successful scheme to operate regular trainloads of canned goods for Libby, McNeil & Libby from Blackwall to Ponders End using former Tube wagons;
a large volume of forwarded scrap traffic from Blackwall, the North London line depots and Instone lines at Bow Creek;
trainloads of imported timber for James Davies (Timber) Ltd to a depot on a stub of the old Midlands & South West (M&SW) route at Swindon;
the bulk movement of sand from Southminster to the old Spitalfields yard;
two new express freight services labelled the *Lea Valley Enterprise*, which started from Waltham Cross, and the *Essex Enterprise*, which originated at Colchester.

Where is the Urinal?

During this period I was nominated for the four-week middle management course held at the School of Transport at Derby from 6 April to 8 May 1964. This was an interesting and useful event rounded off with a coach tour of the Peak District, during which I discovered among my fellow members an astounding repertoire of rugby songs! Another change from the normal routine was an invitation to the annual dinner of the Southern Scrap Association, an event at which it seemed no expense was spared and where, despite the haze of smoke from the cigars, comedian Ted Ray cracked his rapid-fire jokes and played his trademark violin.

The ongoing organisational changes now moved me to the headquarters post of market intelligence officer, reporting to commercial manager, Harry Kinsey. My new boss was a delightful character with an exceptional command of the English language and a habit of using it to the full in everyday communication. If the grapevine was to be believed, even he had been confounded in this propensity during a visit to the London docks. Looking round on his own, he had asked a docker, 'Whereabouts is the urinal?'

The reply was simply, 'I don't know, mate. Which line does she sail for?'

After an interesting tour of my old LT&S line routes, standing in for George Stoddard and in the officers' saloon with General Manager D.S.M. Barrie, I moved on again, this time to the King's Cross Division.

FREIGHT SALES OFFICER, DIVISIONAL MANAGER'S OFFICE, KING'S CROSS 🐾

A Line Saved

From 10 August 1964 to 22 May 1967, I occupied this MS5 post with a starting salary of £2,175 p.a. It was curious to now have responsibilities that included the area in which I had started my career some twenty years earlier. The whole Peterborough district was now part of my patch and its displaced district manager now reported to me. Not that this was a problem, for Reggie Gamble was a most likeable and amiable man, noted for his BBC talks on bee-keeping and well loved in the Peterborough area for the constant fund of stories he was able to deliver in the broad tones of his native Norfolk. These, I remember, included one about an old Norfolk man selling his house on the cliffs at Cromer to two young ladies. Shown the old-fashioned privy at the bottom of the garden, they queried the fact that it had no lock. 'Well,' said the old fellow, 'nothing's ever been stolen from it while I've lived here!'

My new divisional manager was R.H.N. Hardy, a highly experienced and much-loved ex-motive power man who had risen through the difficult

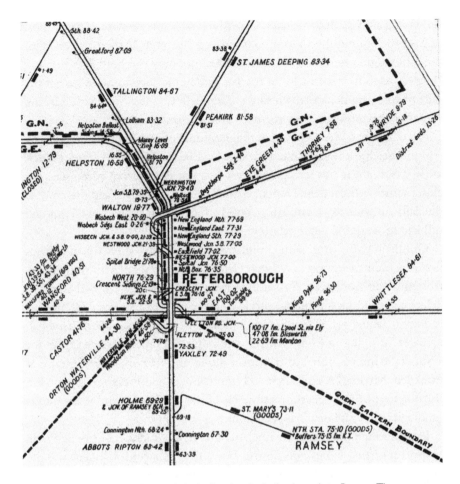

The railways around Peterborough, including the single-line branch to Ramsey. There were extensive brickyards beside the line at Eye, Whittlesea and on the main line south to Yaxley.

route of managing the loco depots at Stratford and Nine Elms. Friendly and fair, Dick Hardy was supported by Edwin Howell as his top operating man, Geoff Wilson as the commercial manager, myself and Rodney Meadows managing freight and passenger sales respectively, and other stalwarts like Bill Stirling, Stephen Howard and Jim Burnham.

The job involved several periods of staff consultation, usually associated with closure or rationalisation schemes. King's Cross Goods Depot was a fairly constant source of difficulty and a close watch had to be kept on the deliveries of fruit and vegetables to the London markets, still quite a substantial activity in those days. One of my sales representatives spent most of his time among the Covent Garden and Borough Market traders. This brought another reminder of the past when not only had both St Neots and Biggleswade still loaded a lot of market garden produce to London, but my wife Sheila's family had grown some of it. Their 'Quince's Red String Beans' were in constant demand by many fashionable restaurants.

A few months after I arrived at the divisional offices in the Euston Road, regional headquarters suggested we should close the Holme–Ramsey branch as they thought it was losing money. I was not prepared to agree without closer scrutiny. In fact, the branch, virtually run by one man and the crew of the daily freight trip, was making a good contribution above direct costs and still had some traffic potential, so we were able to say 'no'.

Our main traffic originating points were King's Cross itself, the numerous firms, including Nabisco, at Welwyn Garden City, and the Peterborough area. Abbots Wood Wool made forwardings from New Southgate, as did Standard Telephone & Cables, while we carried a lot of plastic pipes from the Stewart & Lloyds factory at Huntingdon. A new business I was able to establish involved bringing in from Grimsby the imported food produce intake for a Superior International distribution depot and its new private siding at Buckden. My ex-TA colleague and long-time friend Freight Assistant Jim Burnham must have been heartily sick of me hounding him when transit times fell below the firm's expectations.

Peterborough was especially important to us, its goods depot run by Frank Markham carting in business from as far away as Stamford. Adjacent was the huge General Post Office (GPO) sorting office and a warehouse dealing with the agreed flat-rate business of the Freemans mail order company. The former Peterborough East station became a sorting and staging point for smaller consignments in BRUTES.

A Joke on the Boss

Because of this importance, I arranged a sales conference at Peterborough to explain our business objectives to my team of sales people and others concerned. The venue was the Great Northern Hotel, still with the outbuilding which I had used for storing my bicycle when I had first joined the old LNER. The conference went well and Dick Hardy was kind enough to provide a little note with praise for the affair. This prompted a bit of guilt on my part, for I had played a trick on him on the day of the conference.

My boss never lost his love of locomotives and their crews, and footplate staff held him in very high esteem. This love even took Dick Hardy on periodical visits to France to drive one of the magnificent Chapelon Pacifics on their runs from Calais to Paris. Anyway, the day before the conference I had spotted the guv'nor joining the footplate of the train I was taking to carry out last-minute checks on our meeting arrangements; he did not see me. Then, as we all subsequently journeyed together to the conference itself, I remarked casually to Geoffrey Wilson, who was travelling with us, that I had heard that Malcolm Southgate, the King's Cross station master, had received a lot of passenger complaints about a jerky and uncomfortable journey they had had the day before. Realising that the train I referred to was the one he'd been handling, my boss looked so upset that I had to confess my deception and apologise!

My obligation to spend a fair amount of time at Peterborough was no hardship, for I had good memories of my boyhood there, including rowing in a former ship's lifeboat on the River Nene, cycling through lovely countryside to Stamford, watching a Hawker Hart biplane test-fire its machine guns at Peterborough aerodrome, a bit of shooting of my own on a friend's farm at Whittlesea, and so on. Back then, I'd always been fascinated by the extensive brickyards which stretched alongside the main railway line south as far as the first station at Yaxley & Farcet, clay pits on one side and kilns on the other. Now the London Brick Company (LBC), which had inherited all the former individual yards, was one of my most important clients. Of the 16 million bricks produced every week, we carried just over a quarter.

I was privileged to be shown round the LBC Beebys' brickyard in December 1965 and was able to observe the whole brick-making process. Quarried by excavator, the raw clay passed in small trucks to the crushing mills adjacent to the kilns. There the clay was pressed four times – the origin of the brand name Phorpres – and moved on by conveyor belt to stacks, separate ones for facing bricks and common bricks. Inside the kilns, with their brick arches set along four sides of a rectangle and each with a small fireplace, the brick moulds were heated by gradually lifting the temperature to 1,000°C over a four-day cycle. Once cooled, our consignments of finished facing bricks were then loaded to Shock wagons and the common bricks to ordinary Hyfits, ready for movement to the exchange sidings and collection from there by our local trip working.

At that time we moved regular daily trainloads of London's rubbish from Ashburton Grove to landfill sites along the Hatfield branch. It was not to be long before that huge LBC activity at Peterborough would come to an end and the vast clay pits be used for the same purpose.

A Truly Remarkable Railway

Along the main line north of Peterborough, another important traffic forwarder was Dowsett-Mackay, which despatched its concrete products from a works at Tallington. Concrete sleepers left there in their hundreds with huge bridge beams represented a rather more complicated periodical challenge. There was also a movement of sand traffic from the Helpston area, but the really big business emanated from a mineral-line branch which many a northbound main-line passenger emerging from Stoke Tunnel would not even have noticed.

Opened progressively to Stainby in 1920 and extended to Sproxton in 1923, the High Dyke mineral branch was the source of a constant stream of trains hauling mineral wagons loaded with iron ore to the furnaces at Scunthorpe. Quite apart from the significance of this traffic in revenue terms, my father had been sent to work there quite early in his career and I had long wanted to visit the line. In this I was fortunate in having District Inspector Peter Keys as my guide, for he had once been a signalman at Colsterworth and thus knew the line intimately. My visit was anything but a disappointment, for the single-line route was full of curves, gradients, siding connections and other physical features that rendered its daily operation both unusual and frequently challenging.

We travelled by car to the exchange sidings just south of Grantham and joined the brake van of a train of empties headed by a Brush diesel. Past the underground workings at Burton Lane we came to Colsterworth, where the locomotive came off and moved into a siding while its train was held on the downward slope by the guard's brake. Once the diesel was clear, our headless train was allowed to run down the dip and up the other side, where it was again held by the guard. Out came the locomotive and took its place, and the empty wagons duly ran down to join it and could then be propelled back into the mine sidings. It was an unusual, but fully effective bit of shunting.

The local management kindly arranged for me to be shown the main features of the mining operations, including the work of the huge 25-ton grab excavating ore at Colsterworth and then be taken on by Land Rover to the Easton underground mine. There the extraction process involved cutting downward-sloping tunnels in groups of three, pumping out the sludge as each section was cut and then blasting out the ore between the sections.

This was then removed by a clearance elevator at the rate of some 600 tons per hour.

The High Dyke branch was railway operation at its most down-to-earth. Moving the heavy outward trains of 16-ton mineral wagons demanded much of the 2-8-0 Class O2 locomotives which diesels were replacing. The trains needed a good run down each dip in the route to avoid stalling on the following climb and then a number of brakes pinned down on the final descent to the main line.

Peter Keys was later to describe his experiences on the High Dyke branch in an excellent article in a railway magazine. He recalled the use of prisoners of war to free the line from snow in order to keep the vital ore traffic moving. A subsequent piece on the same subject described an experiment in which a jet aeroplane engine was tried for the same snow clearance purpose. Bolted onto the bed of a flat wagon, the engine was fired up and propelled towards a banked-up snowdrift. Dramatically, but unfortunately, it was so powerful that it set fire to the line's wooden sleepers and any other combustible items in its path. Colsterworth signal box itself only just escaped a similar fate.

SENIOR MANAGEMENT COURSE NO. 16 AT WOKING 📫

During my time in the King's Cross Division I was detached to attend the prestigious senior management course held at the British Transport Staff College at Woking. This lasted eight weeks from 8 May to 5 August 1966, during which the course members endured intensive lectures, seminars and study periods to produce reports and give assessments on a variety of business and management topics. The principal of the college was Pat Cook and the secretary Colonel Claud Lincoln, both formidable administrators as well as skilled players of croquet and liar dice! Each course had some thirty members, representative of all departments and leavened by a few railwaymen from other countries, in our case Canada and Belgium.

Business games and public speaking featured in the syllabus, the latter in the hands of a visiting expert who proved quite merciless, reducing one of our members to tears as part of curing his stammer. Mid-course there was an overseas visit, in our case embracing Schiphol Airport and a Utrecht road haulier specialising in the carriage of clothing on racks. After visiting the latter, the group's singing on the return Amsterdam tram was so good that we did a second circuit by popular request! With a full programme of activities and then a tired return on a ferry offering duty-free Geneva, the pitiful group groping their way ashore at Harwich looked anything but high-potential managers!

Despite a full timetable and a forbidding reading list back in the college, we found time for a croquet tournament and a small syndicate intent on mastering the fruit machine. In the former I lost the final to the principal, but in the latter we were sufficiently successful to be rewarded at a rate of about 19d an hour! Our Canadian member roped me into a barbershop quartet, another late-hours activity. There was also preparation for the traditional end-of-course entertainment, which proved to be ribald in the extreme and embraced reworded traditional songs and a parody of the 'assessment' process, in which we students appraised our tutors. My 'owl poster', based on caricaturing each course member as an owl perched in the branches of a tree – the owl being the college symbol – was later framed and hung in the building.

ACTING DIVISIONAL COMMERCIAL MANAGER, LIVERPOOL STREET 🖾

From 22 May to 11 December 1967 I occupied this position while the incumbent, John Dickinson, was seconded to wind up the ER headquarters offices in London ready for the move to York. On 16 June, I was actually appointed sales promotion officer in the new set-up there, but that move was delayed and eventually overtaken by one to Bristol. Meantime I continued as acting DCM, getting on well with gruff but likeable Divisional Manager W.A.G. Suddaby and Divisional Movements Manager David Cobbett, and taking full commercial control of the division, including reversing some my predecessor's decisions that I thought highly suspect. Activities were varied and ranged from tours with General Manager Derek Barrie in his saloon to opening travel agents' courses. Less happy were duties like visiting rail accident victims in hospital or attending the funeral of a staff member.

Throughout the 1960s, living in Enfield and working in London had provided us with a normal and happy home life. We had made a lot of friends and maintained a close connection with the church, although I had given up my lay preaching. Sheila was involved with its community work, a direction that was eventually to lead to a career as a qualified social worker. One of her voluntary commitments in Enfield was with an organisation that provided accommodation for pregnant women who had no other support. They were a lovely bunch but I had mixed feelings about being roped in frequently to provide transport. Having four or five pregnant young women emerge from one's car could, and did, tend to result in odd looks from bystanders!

MARKETING & SALES MANAGER, WEST OF ENGLAND DIVISION, WR BRISTOL 🚩

All the study, training, extended hours and family life sacrifices paid off handsomely when I was allocated a senior officer position in the West of England Division, based at Bristol. My appointment was one of the moves in a concerted plan to shake the Western Region (WR) out of the remaining vestiges of a period in which the old GWR feudalism and privilege lingered on in some quarters and was hindering the changes needed by the modern railway.

From 11 December 1967 to 16 November 1970, I occupied the SO1 post of Marketing & Sales Manager for Henry Sanderson's West of England Division, located in Transom House, Victoria Street, Bristol. The assistant divisional managers were Clive Rowbury and Ken Painter, and my opposite number was Divisional Movements Manager Bill Bradshaw. Reporting to me were passenger and freight section chiefs Richard Titball and Eric Shaw respectively, the public relations officer Fred Aldgate, a large team of sales representatives and a small presence at Plymouth. The old district office there had been embraced in our new West of England Division, leaving just George Willis as the area marketing man, a PRO and a secretary. My deputy was Commercial Manager Hugh Bunting, soon to retire and be replaced by Leslie Bracey, of whom more later. In addition, the rapidly growing limestone business from the Mendips justified creating the new post of 'Stone Project Manager', who would report to me – this was David Butcher.

The first month or so was taken up with an induction period at Paddington headquarters, a couple of weeks travelling around the division getting to know the area, and then devising a new commercial organisation to fulfil my remit to revitalise my predecessor's unsatisfactory regime. I had noticed that the large metal desk in my new office was marked with the rings left by bottles and glasses, and decided that a clean-up was warranted not only there, but also in the structuring of my support sections.

A Great Variety

What an incredibly rich and interesting mixture this new stamping ground represented. It was a combination of the old Gloucester, Bristol, Exeter and Plymouth districts and thus comprised the Oxford–Hereford line, the NE–SW route south of the Lickey Incline, the Paddington–Bristol/South Wales route from east of Swindon to the Severn Tunnel, the West of England main line from Pewsey, the old L&SW line from Yeovil to Exeter (later partially singled), the Bristol–Warminster/Weymouth lines and the whole of the south-west peninsula as far as Penzance. The passenger stations on these lines and their various branches originated 10 million journeys every year and required a fleet of 76 DMU power cars and 100 main-line diesel-hauled trains, which ranged from the St Ives branch shuttle to named services like *The Mayflower*, the *Golden Hind* and the *Cornish Riviera Express* as well as the Penzance sleepers and car carrier and the Bristol Pullman. In 1966–67 the 709 vans forwarded with Scilly/Cornish flowers and vegetables earned £38,100 and passenger parties rose from 1,136 for £55,898 in 1968 to 1,412 for £69,221 in 1969. Mystery trains and charter trains were also major features.

The freight traffic was also considerable and varied – china and ball clay from Cornwall to the port of Fowey and the potteries; milk in tank wagons from several West Country creameries and Bason Bridge siding;

The special train created at Newton Abbot to operate an overnight Railair Express Parcels service from Bristol to Hayes to connect with flights from Heathrow Airport.

stone from ARC Whatley Quarry and Yeoman's at Dulcote and Merehead; trains of animal feeding stuffs from Avonmouth to Cornwall and West Wales; chemicals from ICI Severnside to Immingham and the North-East; oil from Esso's tank farm at Avonmouth; car body parts from Swindon and so on. From other sidings and freight concentration depots came bananas ex ship at Avonmouth, chocolate products from Fry's at Keynsham, tobacco ex the Wills factories and mail order traffic from Kay's of Worcester. There were numerous inward flows including tin plate for Metal Box, Worcester and coal to Portishead power station and to coal concentration depots like those at Cheltenham, Filton and Wapping Wharf. Parcels traffic was extensive, so much so that on 1 October 1969 we launched a DMU conversion as the Railair Express for the carriage of urgent traffic to Heathrow Airport.

Disaster

In addition to the commercial negotiations associated with keeping and developing these traffic flows, the job embraced public relations functions, liaison with travel agents, various public meetings and press conferences, service improvements, alterations and closures, development of passenger travel centres, new ticketing schemes and much else.

So much for the basic picture. That it would involve an intense and exciting variety I was to find out pretty quickly. Hardly had I met everyone and grasped the essentials than my boss, Sandy, roped me into the panel fielding questions in a Town Forum at Worcester, with another following shortly after at Truro. I needed my wits about me on both occasions. And the saloon tours with General Manager Lance Ibbotson were no easier, for he could, and did, question everything he saw. Thankfully I had done a considerable amount of homework before each.

A major emergency occurred in July 1968. I had been aware of the heavy rain which had been falling in Bristol all day, but as I was engrossed in other matters, it was not until Control called me at home in the evening that I became aware of the train problems that were beginning to mount up. In the Control Office I was to find Maurice Holmes with a hand-drawn map of the lines around Bristol, on which he had begun to record the lines blocked by flooding, the trains stranded and a variety of other troubles. That process was to continue for another twenty-four hours, in which all our ingenuity was needed to rescue stranded passengers and provide them with food, shelter and help with other needs. When, at last, the downpour abated and the waters began to recede, we had to tackle the mess, with staff travelling on

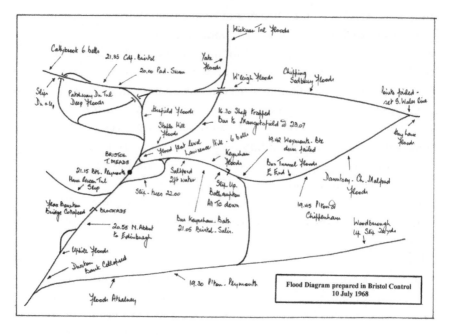

Hand-drawn map used in the Bristol Control Office to record the dramatic impact of the July 1968 heavy rain on the rail network.

light engines to check that blocked lines were again clear and often having to remove debris in the process. It took a long while and a lot of effort to clear up the devastation and get back to normal.

Pumping Engines and Monkey Specials

The six saloon tours of 1968 included one especially memorable visit, that to Sudbrook pumping station. The 72ft beams of the Cornish engines which had kept the Severn Tunnel drained of 20 million gallons of water or more each day had just been replaced by impeller pumps, but they were magnificent, even in repose. And the descent to the lowest level and walk along the grating covering the rushing flow of the Great Spring was another major experience, capped by emerging into the noise, darkness and atmosphere of mid-tunnel. Trains thundered past just a couple of feet away.

In those days, when coaching stock was more plentiful, we worked hard to develop the special train business. We organised a programme of Mystery Trains to cater for a surprisingly large clientele who liked the excitement of not knowing where they were headed. I learned that one couple planned to celebrate their ruby wedding anniversary with one of these Mystery Train trips and, with PRO Fred Aldgate's able assistance in getting the media interested, presented them with a special cake on the journey.

The South Wales staff sent us regular 'Monkey Specials' which ran to Clifton Downs station, where passengers alighted for a visit to Bristol Zoo. From the London Division we received special trains designed to persuade people to spend holidays in the West of England by offering a day visit at a cheap fare to enable them to see its attractions. One such train with a call booked at Teignmouth was to be met by representatives of the local hoteliers and tourist bodies, but unfortunately the driver omitted the stop and continued towards Torbay. A disaster, we thought, until Leslie Bracey hurried down there and, with his usual rather cheeky humour, convinced the angry local dignitaries that they had received more publicity from the train not stopping than would have accrued if all had gone as planned!

The Wild West

I had previously thought of Cornwall only in holiday terms. Now it was an important source of traffic for us, a fact that the chairman of the county council hammered home at a lunch he invited us to. Clive Rowbury and I were the only guests and were astonished to find the event quite lavish, as if we were visiting nobility who needed to be impressed with the importance of the man and what he represented – plenty of silverware, candles and the like. Our host was right in his overall message and I became deeply involved with the massive china clay business, meeting English China Clays regularly to discuss the rates and operating arrangements for servicing the complex network of mineral lines in the area between Burngullow and St Denis Junction. The key location was the yard and loco depot at St Blazey, which fed the empty Hyfits and standard open wagons to the various loading sidings, then marshalled the outwards ones when they were tripped back to St Blazey. The export forwardings were then hauled to Carne Point for shipment under an arrangement which gave us a good volume of business in return for allowing one of the two Fowey branches to be converted and used for road movements.

In September 1968 I visited the Scilly Isles, flying by helicopter from Penzance airport to St Mary's for a meeting with the Isles of Scilly Steamship Company, which acted as our agent on the islands. The company's vessel, the

Wagons of china clay worked in from St Blazey are being tipped to vessel at Fowey.

Scillonian, carried the early daffodils grown in the Scillies' temperate climate over to Penzance for rail forwarding from there. The main discussions took place in the evening of my arrival, once I had been to my hotel to book in. A very nice meal was provided in a private room in the company's offices and my host was helpful, genial and then generous with his brandy afterwards. I don't think it impaired my rate negotiations, but I was somewhat less sharp-witted than usual as I finally left the premises, just before ten o'clock. What I did not know was that all the street lights in St Mary's went out at ten, before I had taken more than a few steps. Finding my hotel in a strange town in near total darkness and with my wits dulled was an interesting exercise.

It was foggy the next day and the return helicopter flight was cancelled. I rang May, the secretary at Plymouth, explained that this put me at the back of the subsequent queue for flights and asked her to let our Bristol HQ know the position. I mentioned that if there was fog every second day, I could apparently stay there at British Rail expense for a long time – my idea of humour. She later rang back and said, 'Mr Rowbury says you're not to worry about it.' Very generous of him, I thought, but later learned he had told May, 'Tell him if he's not back in two days, we'll advertise his job.' This was *his* sense of humour, which May was too kindly a soul to pass on unedited.

Clive Rowbury and I attended a meeting with the Cornish broccoli growers to discuss rates and train services for the next growing season. As always, and understandably, their goal was the latest possible loading times along with rates that would match those of geographically nearer growers, but which overlooked the longer distances we had to haul the trainloads of laden vans from Carn Brea and Marazion to London and the other markets. As the evening wore on, those attending seemed to forget Clive and me in a local dispute between the National Farmers' Union (NFU) faction and the non-NFU group. We listened fascinated for a while, but then crept out quietly and left them to it.

Later I did my own personal study and report on the potential of this business as a guide to our sales tactics and service provision. It was not long before I found that the Ministry of Agriculture's crop figures were quite unreliable because the independent Cornish spirit was not keen on any sort of bureaucratic involvement in local affairs.

Bad and Good at Ashchurch

In March 1969 there was a fatal rail crash at Ashchurch. A southbound coal train suffered a derailment just as the 10.40 a.m. Bristol to Newcastle express was passing, and some of the coal wagons sliced into the side of the rear coaches of the passenger train. Two people were killed and thirty-four injured, involving me in distressing hospital visits to check on their condition and needs. More positive was a later study I burned midnight oil over to check on my suspicion that the closed Ashchurch station had more passenger traffic potential than had been realised. It seemed to me to be in the centre of a very large catchment area, and demonstrating this was a factor in its later reopening.

More Personal

With such a large and complex area to manage commercially, my job was always going to be pretty demanding, but there were many compensations. Bristol was a pleasant city to live in with ample facilities and there was easy access to places like Bath, the Forest of Dean, Somerset's coast and the Mendip, Blackdown, Quantock and Brendon Hills. We could as easily go to the theatre in Cardiff as we could previously get from Enfield into the heart of London. My drive to work each day was alongside the River Avon, often with a sand boat or other vessel to keep me company. Our social life was good too, partly because Sandy encouraged his senior staff to host Sunday coffee mornings, which led on to Sheila and I often having dinner with Bill and Jill Bradshaw at Bradford-on-Avon and them with us in Westbury-on-Trym.

We did have the occasional foreign holiday but, with the West Country so handy, we used to take self-catering breaks on Exmoor and at places like Looe, Newton Ferrers and Cawsands. Returning from the latter, we were able to arrange to travel with Plymouth chauffeur Ron Hodges who had to come up to Bristol. No wrestling with luggage, I thought, until Clive Rowbury asked if we would also bring back his dog, down there for some reason I no longer recall. The journey did, however, prove memorable. Sheila and the two boys occupied the rear bench seat of the Ford Zephyr with Ron in the driver's position on the front one, myself by the window and the boxer dog in between. Lulled by the driving rhythm, the rather large boxer soon leaned over, pressing me against the door, and promptly dropped off to sleep. Seeming to get heavier and heavier, he refused to straighten up and could hardly be pushed over to lean on Ron. From time to time he would dribble amiably on me or give me a friendly lick with a huge tongue. The whole business seemed highly amusing to those in the back seat!

More saloon tours were undertaken in 1969 and 1970, along with open days at Worcester and St Blazey. Sheila and I were among the hosts who escorted a group of senior mayors from Cornwall and Devon to London in readiness for their more formal journey back to celebrate improved services in May 1969. It was also in 1969 that we decided to use the services of the Welcome Wagon, which provided small promotional gifts for people moving into the area. This coincided with Leslie Bracey retiring and Trevor Anderson taking his place, buying a house near Thornbury and moving in there prior to his wife Diane joining him. With the help of the Welcome Wagon supervisor, we arranged to visit him armed with a bottle of champagne held by a very attractive young lady – the supervisor's daughter – seated in an oversize basket. Trevor's response to this parody of the usual welcome was a moment of astonishment and then the reaction, 'Can I keep her?'

Ever since my early article on the Essendine–Bourne branch had been published in *Trains Illustrated* and earned me the princely sum of £2, I had been writing articles for railway and county magazines. There had been small booklets too and my long-running link with David & Charles, for whom I edited the annual *Light Railway Guide & Timetables*, now moved on to an acceptance for publication of my first full-sized work, on the subject of (and to be called) *British Paddle Steamers*.

'Now Let's See Your Ticket'

As the year reached its end, I did a formal press conference signing of a contract with Renwick's travel agents to provide them with twenty-seven charter trains. A similar freight event had been held before when the contract was with Rio Tinto Zinc at the firm's Avonmouth plant. The traffic variety around the Port of Bristol Authority's Avonmouth docks ranged from imported ore for this firm to regular imports of bananas. The latter passed in ventilated vans with dry ice to prevent the fruit ripening before the 'hands' reached the ripening sheds in Lincolnshire. Great care was need in loading to avoid poisonous spiders, which were likely to be out of temper after their involuntary journey from Central America.

This period had been strongly affected by the multiple-aspect signalling scheme for Bristol, which caused a fair amount of disruption of normal services, all of which had to be explained to our passengers and the effect minimised as far as possible. The result would allow much greater operational flexibility at Temple Meads. Our service to passengers was also enhanced by the opening of Bristol Parkway, designed to lure business away from the nearby M4 motorway.

Somewhat different was the branch-line passenger activity, which included the short route from Maiden Newton to Bridport. John Palette, who had replaced Henry Sanderson when the latter moved to the BR Board, decided he wanted to weigh up the branch's value first-hand and asked me to accompany him. On the shuttle DMU from Maiden Newton, John showed the conductor guard the medallion that was accorded to the most senior staff and represented their authority to travel anywhere. This was clearly something of a mystery on this remote little line, for the response was, 'That's nice. Now let's see your ticket.'

In addition to the time I spent on internal matters, including being roped in by Staff Officer Ron Bateman to make retirement, first aid and Best Kept Station presentations, my job involved a great deal of liaison with outside people and agencies. It was a bonus that the three WR divisional marketing and sales managers, Brian Minks at Reading, David Jagoe at Cardiff and myself at Bristol, got on so well that we could react collectively to the worthwhile headquarters initiatives, yet have a combined voice sufficient to reject the occasional rogue idea. My duties also included liaison with the major bus companies. One of these was the Devon General, which generously invited Sheila and me to join its senior staff on the annual river trip up the Tamar with a strawberry tea provided.

The links with water transport were also quite numerous, not just the dock activity at Plymouth, Teignmouth, Penzance, Fowey, Fremington and Bristol itself, but also arranging facilities or combined excursions with Campbell's steamers, the River Dart vessel operators and the Exmouth Dock company, which also provided the ferry link between Exmouth and Starcross, where the ferry terminal adjoined our station. A curious water connection arose when the local authority asked us to postpone the closure of the river bridge link from the former GWR station at Barnstaple to Barnstaple Town because of problems caused by temporary flooding.

The Pop Music Affair

Not long after our Tamar trip we had to react quickly or be badly caught out by a totally unexpected event. Quite out of the blue, news started coming through of extraordinary numbers of mainly young people leaving Paddington and intent on travelling into the heart of Somerset. What was later to grow into the massive Glastonbury music festival was about to be born at Pilton, but had been publicised only in music circles. We did our best to help those alighting at Bath and hurriedly began planning for the subsequent return of numbers sure to be both exciting and daunting.

Bill Bradshaw and his team elected to focus on Castle Cary station on the West of England main line and we made arrangements for the police to direct the returning fans there. I gathered as many of my staff as I could and headed down to this modest junction with the Weymouth line. Once there, we increased the number of ticketing points by removing several windows in the booking office, manned them and then prepared for the onslaught as the mass of fans appeared on foot, in coaches, by taxi and so on. By using ticketing machines to book people waiting in line in the huge queues, we fed the platforms at a rate the modest station had never before witnessed. There Bill and his team were playing havoc with the timetable by arranging to stop anything heading east and loading it with as many appropriate passengers as could be squeezed on. In the midst of all this, a couple of Reading travelling ticket inspectors decided they wanted to check everyone's tickets, which would have led to chaos. I sent them home.

Returning pop festival fans at Castle Cary station in 1970.

Robbie Burns's 1786 comment on 'the best laid schemes o' mice an' men' going 'aft a-gley' proved appropriate for our attempts to make capital out of the return of the SS *Great Britain* to Bristol in 1970. After successfully completing the hazardous journey from the Falkland Islands to Avonmouth, the plan was to tow the historic vessel up the River Avon to Bristol on a suitable tide and then berth her in the dry dock where restoration was to take place. With our Portishead line running for some way along the south bank of the river, this seemed too good a promotional opportunity to miss, so we commandeered one of the Blue Pullman sets and invited important traders and folk of influence to travel on it to witness the momentous upriver journey. Unfortunately, something went wrong with the vessel movement plan and we were left with a train full of guests deprived of the expected spectacle, which had been postponed. So we took them on a tour of all the lines around Bristol and trusted to the ongoing supply of champagne to ease their disappointment.

Turned to Stone

Not everything in the Division went well, of course. My Railair Express was not paying its way and had to be terminated, Freightliner's mini-terminals at Par, Plymouth and Bristol were not attracting enough new business, and there had been a lot of teething problems on the former Southern Region (SR) Exeter–Salisbury route, where the partial line singling took a while to settle down. Nursed by project managers David Butcher and then Peter Nicholls, one business had been growing steadily all the time I had been at Bristol, that of Mendip stone despatched by rail to meet the demands of the growing motorway network. Passing in trainloads from the Foster Yeoman Mendip Hills quarry at Dulcote and ARC's Whatley Quarry, the business was now about to grow even further with the opening of a new rail-connected terminal at Merehead. I was fortunate enough to be among the Yeoman guests invited for the opening ceremony, which included a tour of the impressive plant. The primeval force displayed in sound and sparks as the huge blocks of stone went into the maw of the crusher seemed to defy

Diesel hydraulic locomotive D1022 heads a trainload of stone in Foster Yeoman's newly opened railhead at Merehead, near Frome.

the senses, and I found myself glad of the steadying feel of the protective rail around the viewing platform.

A Move and a Bucket

The general expectation was that senior staff like myself would not stay in a position more than about three years. Truth to tell, I was nervous about the risk of being forced to return to London and, in any event, felt ready for a 'command' of my own. I also liked living in Bristol, so when the post of South West area manager for Freightliners, with an office in the city, came up, I decided to apply – successfully, as it turned out.

There were many regrets at leaving the WR West of England Division, such a rich and interesting territory, and fine colleagues. The three years there had honed my character, widened my understanding and produced many outstanding memories, not just the dramas like the Bristol area floodings, the Ashchurch crash and the Pilton pop festival, but also many more personal ones. The latter ranged from the camaraderie that had us out on summer Saturdays, keeping an eye on the holiday train workings, to being presented with a genuine period GWR toilet seat at one of our annual dinners, in a gentle dig at my habit of collecting railway relics and ephemera. We took our job seriously, but laughed when we could, like the occasion at the morning conference when George Robson was reporting the damage to a train which had struck a bucket of ballast that had been left in the 'four foot' between the rails. Long was the list of the scars, pipes and couplings disturbed, battery boxes damaged and so on. As the list ended, Dan Reynolds added drily, 'And it didn't do the bucket any good either!'

AREA MANAGER (SOUTH WEST), FREIGHTLINERS LIMITED 🖙

The Terminals

Enough looking back; I now looked forward to the new activity and its challenges. A major bonus was not having to move home from our house in the Westbury-on-Trym suburb of Bristol. I had done a twelve-year stint in London, had tasted better things and wanted no more of that. Fortune was with me in that the vacancy in this Freightliner position in Bristol arose while David Cobbett was acting as that company's managing director. I had worked for David when he was chief controller at Liverpool Street and we

Trailers from the Cardiff (Pengam) Freightliner terminal await a load of Israeli oranges at Cardiff Docks.

got on well. No doubt this helped, for I got the job and moved the short distance to new offices rented on the seventh floor of Tower House in the city centre.

My headquarters team was modest in size and included deputy Ron Dunn and staff man Bryan Hire. Half a dozen others occupied the main office, with the two secretaries in their own room adjacent to mine. The area had three terminals, at Cardiff (Pengam), Swansea (Dan-y-Graig) and Southampton (Millbrook), each with its own container collection and delivery fleet, road motor servicing depot, transfer sidings and overhead cranes, and with a small terminal building for the terminal manager and his clerical and operational staff. Each did a fair amount of varied and profitable business.

Dick Scarley was the terminal manager at Southampton (Millbrook) terminal, located on the Up side of the approach lines to Southampton Central, parallel with the dock area, which in turn paralleled it on the Down side. Dick was a likeable and very able railwayman, honed in the tough school of operating the intensive passenger services on the SR's routes in Kent. His reminiscences of working the trains containing the hop pickers and their weekend visiting families were hair-raising, with so much misuse of the communication cord that in extreme cases the train brake pipes had to be disconnected altogether. Dick and I had a good working relationship and some pleasant and productive outings, like the flight over from Bournemouth to Guernsey to negotiate with the Tomato Board there.

Lost at Sea?

Much of Millbrook's business was in shipping traffic, containers of import and export goods hauled between the terminal and the docks. A major customer on the inwards side was the Dart Line, which not only performed the deep-sea movement but also negotiated with us for the delivery of inwards flows moved by our trains to inland destinations. My contact was Captain Peter Doble, whom I entertained regularly at the Dolphin Hotel in Southampton and who kindly invited me to some of the amazing lunches he was able to offer on board ship.

Another nice gesture I received was an offer to be shown around one of the Dart Line container vessels, something I accepted with alacrity. Peter was not able to take me round himself, but deputed one of the company's visiting London office staff to do so. It was an impressive experience, but remarkable for the fact that the sophisticated handling and storage of standardised containers and the modern, computerised ship control systems meant that in the labyrinth below the main deck we did not see another soul.

When the tour ended, somewhere in the bowels of the huge vessel, I noticed that my guide was less relaxed than he had been earlier. The reason became clearer when, quite innocently, I asked what time the ship was due to sail. Sheepishly, he revealed that we had only a little over half an hour to disembark, which would have been ample if my guide had had any idea of how to get 'topside' again or if there had been anyone about to ask. At one stage my vivid imagination had conjured up a call I might later have to make from the ship-to-shore radio room, explaining to my wife that we were just off the coast of southern Ireland and was there anything I could bring her back from New York! Blundering about, ever upward, fortunately avoided that necessity, but it was a close-run thing.

A Brand New Depot

Dick Scarley's right-hand man at Southampton was Jack Wickens, who was used as our on-site operating representative for the building of a new terminal there to deal with the expanding maritime business. He did an excellent job, which was warmly acknowledged at an opening event with principals OCL and ACT at Botley Grange in June 1972. Freightliner's new managing director, Leslie Leppington, had officiated when we had earlier seen off the first train from this new Southampton (Maritime) terminal, which was located on the Down side of the main line west of the older Millbrook. The installation used some very impressive computer technology to control the whole movement of containers from ship's hold to transfer tug and then to rail cranes. All loads were dropped expertly onto the waiting flat wagons, twist locks were carefully secured and the driver then received the signal to move the momentous first train on its way.

Steel and Opera

Cardiff (Pengam) terminal was in the hands of Jim Russell. It too dealt with a considerable amount of business carted to and from the still very active docks, both at Cardiff itself and at Newport. One of the main flows was that of oranges imported under the control of the Citrus Marketing Board of Israel. We managed to get a valuable new contract for this business, which was important enough for the contract to get signed at a ceremony in February 1974 in Cardiff Castle, in the presence of Cardiff's lady mayoress.

The steel business was another vital feature of the Cardiff activity, but posed its own problems. Special flatbed containers were needed for the two main varieties of sheet and coil steel, and the senders, British Steel, were quick to pounce on any risk of movement in transit as this made the steel unsuitable for the industrial use for which it was intended. Guest, Keen & Nettlefold was another of our heavy industry clients with which I had frequent dealings.

My third terminal was on the eastern approaches to Swansea and, again, carried a lot of steel, produced mainly at Port Talbot. Stan Judd was an excellent manager there and enlightened me about a customer relations tradition which I was only too happy to perpetuate. It was the practice to entertain the main South Wales customers to an annual event housed in the former grand home of diva Adelina Patti at Craig-y-Nos in the upper Swansea Valley. The famous singer had lived there in a style befitting her status and could even command her own special railway carriage when she travelled on the local line. Her impressive home had a lovely little theatre seating about fifty people, and with the help of the Neath Opera Group and guest principals we were able to stage an opera production each year for our main clients as a recognition of the business we had been given. Despite my duties as host, I remember with tremendous pleasure the unique experience of savouring performances of *La Bohème* and *The Marriage of Figaro* in such a relaxed and intimate setting. In *La Bohème* it was almost like being in the garret with Mimi and Rodolfo. The interval glass of wine and light food on the terrace overlooking the green valley of the River Tawe in the gathering dusk enhanced the event to almost magical status.

On the personal front, David & Charles published my first hardback book, *British Paddle Steamers*, in 1971 and then commissioned one to be called *Railways for Pleasure*.

Change Happens

In October 1972, I was offered the post of commercial manager at Freightliner headquarters in London, but thankfully Roger Hall the incumbent was able to resume in the post after his period of illness. At this time the Freightliner company was growing closer to the National Freight Corporation (NFC) which, with, British Rail, was its part owner. I found myself involved in private NFC discussion dinners with senior figures like the general secretary of the Trades Union Congress, Len Neal, and the Minister of Transport, Richard Marsh. I was also nominated to the NFC's Management Development Group, attending its sessions at the Manchester Business School. Attendance at a course at the Roffey Park Institute on the 'Human Aspects of Management' was both useful and challenging.

Rationalisation was now in the air for the area management part of Freightliners and it was clear that this middle tier of control was to go. The outcome for me was a successful interview in September 1973, followed by a transfer to the NFC as a prelude to taking up a new position as director and general manager of Pickfords Tank Haulage Ltd from 1 December of that year. This was an exciting promotion into a very different business, but had the pleasant dividend that I would not need to move home as the company's headquarters was located in Stroud, under an hour's journey away.

I had feared before this development that I might be forced by changes in the Freightliner structure to move to the London headquarters or even to leave altogether, and had started thinking about a different career. An approach to Moonraker Press to see if they had any vacancies led instead to a commission to write a book about Bristol's Clifton Suspension Bridge, which entailed a somewhat hair-raising clamber up to the top of one of the approach towers as part of its compilation process. In 1973, Sheila and I also managed to squeeze in a Mediterranean cruise.

ON MY OWN ☞

I was to spend three interesting years in charge of Pickfords Tank Haulage, years that entailed a lot of challenges for a former railwayman in a road transport industry. The Tankfreight group of the National Freight Corporation had two tanker companies within its portfolio: my own Pickfords Tank Haulage and the Heckmondwyke-based Harold Wood Ltd. Their amalgamation was inevitable and came to a head in 1976. Although I was offered the post of operations manager at the new northern headquarters, I had run my own operation for too long to forgo its status and satisfactions, and opted to leave instead. Truth to tell, I liked living in the West Country and was weary of some of the drudgery of big business – politics, regulations, trade union negotiations, etc., all detracting from the more exciting task of operating over 200 road tankers carrying anything from carbon black to imported Italian wine.

At last, I now had the opportunity to set up on my own and develop some previous tentative publishing into something full-time and worthwhile. Railways had always been a passion as well as a job. I had written a number of magazine articles on the subject and self-published booklets on such subjects as the London & Blackwall Railway and the East Anglian Railway. David & Charles, still in the early stages of their own development, published a small work on cliff railways and then *The Light Railway Guide & Timetables*.

Working from my small bedroom study at home in Bristol, I now began a totally new life in a sphere that had so long been close to my heart. From small beginnings I steadily built up my publishing of railway books under the imprint of Avon-AngliA Publications & Services (AAA). This was eventually to produce and market over a hundred titles and undertake many extraneous activities, publicity work for Clearwell Castle in the Forest of Dean, guide books for the Skyfame Aircraft Museum and two railway societies, poster and postcard distribution, and the like.

I began a close association with eminent railway historian Charles Clinker. Preparing his massive 27,000-entry *Register of Closed Stations* for publication to subscribers was a herculean task, but the reprint of his *Leicester & Swannington Railway* could be done quickly and start bringing back some return from the rapid consumption of my Pickfords departure settlement cash. Fortunately my wife was now a fully qualified social worker, so I did not have to live on the meagre profits made in those first publishing years, when capital was needed to expand the AAA book list but returns took some time to materialise.

Rail Link Restored

A strong feature of this new life was to arise from my old connection with BR's Western Region and a liaison with its public relations officers, especially Ron Drummond, which led to a whole list of books designed to explain and raise interest in the region's activities and promoted as the Western at Work series.

The Riviera Express and its Route, *Rail 125 in Action* and *Paddington 1854–1979* were followed by special subject titles in the growing Western at Work series. I had also completed full-sized books: *Railways for Pleasure* for David & Charles and *The Illustrated History of Preserved Railways* for Spur Books. By the end of 1980, I had signed up with Patrick Stephens Ltd for the Field Guide series, major works devoted to revealing the high interest in the multiple aspects of the rail system.

This modest writing and publishing about the industry that was always so important to me in personal interest terms was now my livelihood. With Ian's help, the *Guide to Light Railways* that David & Charles had passed over to me, along with its larger companion *The Railway Enthusiast's Handbook,* was still coming out and was to last for twenty-three editions. It all sounds easy but getting data from multiple sources never is and those were still the days of typesetting, paste-ups and letterset printing. All our advertisers were bent on asking us to squeeze a full page of copy into a half-page space!

The *Advanced Passenger Train* work had been published along with several other small books and some joint productions with other organisations and publishers. Typical of AAA activities was a 3,000 printing of the *Heart of Wales Line* and an arrangement, through the good offices of Cardiff PRO Neil Sprinks, for it to be sold on the Shrewsbury–Swansea trains by members of the Brecon Railway Society. Three reprints were to follow.

In 1981, I signed a contract with Moorland Publishing for *The Railway Era*, which appeared in the following year. However, a lot of my time now had to be spent travelling over the whole of the Western Region gathering material for the first Field Guide, *Railways of the Western Region*, which came out in March 1983. The same marathons preceded the Southern Region volume, which appeared in 1984, and the first part of the Eastern Region coverage, which followed in 1986. The latter, dealing with what had been the original Eastern Region (i.e. south of Doncaster), was truly home territory for me and evoked many memories. All this had to be done while still dealing with the normal book sales business. I had even compounded the workload problem by moving home to Weston-super-Mare and by acquiring a second publishing enterprise, Kingsmead Press, which specialised in local books and art reference works.

Sheep May Safely Graze

On the Western Region, thoughts were now turning to the celebration in 1985 of the 150th anniversary of the Great Western Railway, an even bigger challenge than the Invicta and Rocket occasions. I had now been acting as a publishing publicist for the WR for some five years and enjoyed a very businesslike but friendly relationship with the regional PRO, Ron Drummond. We had concluded an agreement that allowed Avon-AngliA to reprint extracts from the former *GWR Magazine* and market these on a subscription basis. This connection was to lead to my involvement in the GWR150 celebrations, and also to an invitation that was to prove less dramatic but still quite memorable.

The occasion was the launch of the Cotswold & Malvern Express on 14 May 1984. I was invited to join the inaugural run because AAA was to produce another booklet in the Western at Work series, devoted to the Oxford–Hereford line. The guests were representatives of the media and other people of influence, and in a couple of coaches of the spotless high-speed train the usual snacks and drinks had been carefully laid out to impress them.

To link the new service to the communities it was to serve, it had been decided to feature elements of the area's interest on board, the hostesses being in costumes that would have been commonplace in the Civil War era. Events at Worcester and Hereford included a visit to the Bulmer Cider premises at the latter place, an occasion that was to leave the return service short of quite a few of its guest complement! Another idea had been to feature the work of the Rare Breeds Trust at Guiting Power by displaying two of its animals for part of the journey. Unfortunately, the goats that the trust provided proved unused to polite society and had no inhibitions about nibbling the girls' costumes, cadging what they could from the array of snacks and then treating the coach carpets as their personal toilet areas.

THE BIG ANNIVERSARIES 📨

Invicta150

My former opposite number in the WR's London Division was Brian Minks, who moved on to become PRO for the Southern Region. To him fell the task of organising a celebration of the 150th anniversary of the pioneer Canterbury & Whitstable Railway, whose Gala Opening Day had taken place on 3 May 1830. One of its more curious claims to fame was that the railway directors so wanted to have a tunnel on their line that they rejected the flattest, least costly route in favour of a more steeply graded one, necessitating the use of two expensive rope-worked inclines.

Although becoming involved rather late in the day, I was able to contribute by including the commemorative sales items in my Avon-AngliA company sales activity. A pleasant spin-off benefit was an invitation to attend the celebratory events scheduled for Saturday, 3 May 1980, where a civic procession was followed by a service in Canterbury Cathedral and then an outdoor lunch in the adjacent Westgate Gardens. To cater for the latter, tables and folding metal chairs had been positioned, decorated and made ready for the service of what the old opening ceremonies used to call 'a cold collation'.

By this time the overnight rain had thankfully ceased, but the grassed luncheon area was very wet underfoot. It was an unfortunate coincidence that the chairs were of the four-metal-leg variety, so that as the guests sat down the individual legs all tended to sink gently and at varied and unpredictable angles into the sodden ground below. It was a truly comical sight, with astonishment, minor alarm and many exclamations enlivening the occasion, but no great harm was done, all was taken in good part and there was even one thoughtful reference to the biblical advice and that of Dorothy L. Sayers against building a house on sand!

Rocket150

Back in January 1979, my increasingly close links with my BR past had led to a meeting with Paul Watkinson at Euston which, in turn, led to a commission to produce the official handbook for the 1980 Rocket150 celebration of the

150th anniversary of the Liverpool & Manchester (L&M) Railway. This was a big job and a big boost for my small publishing enterprise. Off I went to meet Ken Dixon, the divisional manager at Liverpool, that office being responsible for making the arrangements for the forthcoming events. I knew Ken from my Liverpool Street days and he deputed John Searson and Tony Quirk to give me what help I needed.

Office research done, I went with John Searson to visit Chat Moss and walk the bog which had so sorely tried the original L&M builders. It was still a desolate place, a dead fox hanging from one tree to discourage others. However, we had the excitement of coming across one of the original stone sleepers, which John later arranged to transfer to Liverpool Museum. I did some further research there and at the National Railway Museum, got the text of the book drafted and photographs gathered, and had the whole lot approved and then printed ready for distribution early in the anniversary year. Peter Townsend of Silver Link Publishing helped to swell the sales.

In all their highly polished splendour, the LNER's *Sir Nigel Gresley* and *Flying Scotsman* prepare for their participation in the Rocket 150 locomotive cavalcade.

The L&M's famous Rainhill Trials to determine which locomotive design would be adopted by the new railway were commemorated by a cavalcade of historic and modern locomotives and vehicles in a three-day event at Rainhill on 24–26 May 1980. This was an extremely colourful and memorable occasion preceded by a period in which the cavalcade entrants were gathered together in the sidings of the adjacent National Coal Board's Bold Colliery. Wandering around the arrivals as they were checked, groomed and steamed was, in some ways, an even more memorable experience. Using photographs taken mainly by R.J. Blenkinson over the two periods, and with the London Midland Region's blessing, Avon-AngliA published a 48-page tribute to the whole event entitled *Liverpool & Manchester: A Photographic Essay.* With the help of artist and friend Roy Gallop and the co-operation of Mike Warne of our Wymondham printers, we had this on offer in an incredibly short space of time.

GWR150

Despite being incredibly busy, this period in the 1980s was a happy one for me. We had the sorts of problems all working families have, but it was a good family, living in a nice area and surrounded by very pleasant countryside. Like all social workers, Sheila had pressures, as did I, but we were happy.

For me, that state derived in no small measure from the fact that I was making a living in the world of books, able to apply such literary and marketing skills as I had acquired and yet doing so with a large involvement with the railway industry that was part of my lifeblood. Our new home by the sea was in the lower half of a former Weston-super-Mare town manse where we could spare a large room for my business activity plus the whole of the three-section basement. It was called Annesley House, which was a pleasing coincidence as it shared a name with Annesley Junction, an important location on two routes through the Nottinghamshire coalfields

The experience I had built up of the public interest in railways led to Ron Drummond asking me to Swindon to seek my advice on a railway board game that had been sent to him in the hope of some form of support. It was fascinating and very complex but doomed by needing a huge explanatory booklet. While I was there, Ron also raised with me the subject of the forthcoming anniversary, mentioning that he was getting advice, the nature of which quite horrified me. For the sales facility on the planned exhibition train, the recommendations seemed to me to amount to a sort of travelling Harrods. Now, I knew full well that high-priced

Sheila Body on duty in the sales coach of the GWR150 exhibition train in 1985.

prestige items just would not appeal to the families that would make up the bulk of the visitors. I was later to be proved right when such expensive goods as had already been commissioned sold in small numbers, while the locomotive badges, pencils and other small items I obtained moved in quantity and demanded frequent restocking.

I am not quite sure how it happened but the upshot of this conversation was that I found myself agreeing to undertake the whole commercial aspect of the GWR150 event – sales coach design, sales stock, counter staffing, mail order activities, accounting and, again, arranging an official handbook. The enormity of the task for a virtually one-man business now horrifies me, but then it seemed – and, indeed was – a huge and exciting opportunity. Ian was a great help, as he always had been, and, being in the public relations section at Swindon, made sure that my information was always up-to-date and accurate.

The exhibition train was already being built, using redundant passenger vans, at Cathays Works. So off I went there, clutching my drawings, to instruct the carpenters on what I wanted in terms of glass-fronted exhibition cases, stock shelves, counter area, cash security and a dozen other aspects. Cynically, I suppose, it was so ordered that visitors to the coach could not leave without passing the sales counter and its space for the most popular stock!

Philip Rees, the regional chief civil engineer, started the GWR150 period off with a series of lectures on the Great Western Railway/WR and used these as a basis for writing part of the handbook. I added a second part full of GWR dates, facts and other information. The mail order brochure had already been designed and printed, so I started placing orders with manufacturers, thankful that I had more storage room in Annesley House, the new home, and that genial supervisor Malcolm at Weston-super-Mare station had found me some storage space there. My Kingsmead Press also had warehouse space I could use. The other main task at this period was to enlist my local friends and some of Sheila's to staff the exhibition train as it moved around the main WR towns and cities. Many seemed extraordinarily keen for this, to them, unusual experience. I now had a Toyota HiAce van that I could use for the task of restocking.

The prestige launch of the whole enterprise was based around the exhibition train's first public opening, at Paddington on 29 May 1985. Ian and I had driven up early on the previous day and laboured hard at stocking the display and storage areas where the train was stabled in the fish dock, and I was there again early on the special day. It was a great, full-on success, so much so that I had to get home to Weston and back to stock up again in time for the second day.

And so began the hectic round of the exhibition train tour, which embraced pretty well all the significant locations of the old GWR as far north as Wolverhampton and Shrewsbury and as far west as Aberystwyth and Penzance. Ceremonial openings, the influx of visitors, restocking and tidying up became the pattern, then on to the next location. In the few days in between, I was able to catch up on the mail orders, bank the cash and account for it, organise the increasing number of supplementary activities like the travel centre sales and, of course, pay our suppliers and counter staff.

It all went surprisingly well. There were a few problems, like the one at Barry Island where the only way to resupply the sales coach was to manoeuvre the HiAce alongside and pass the new stock through the tiny, high sliding window. Sheila and Ian made major contributions, as did all the counter staff, stewards, trainmen and station staff. However, in the way that one remembers one's failures more vividly than the successes, I can still feel slightly warm under the collar about the York visit. It was one of the additions made at the end of the main programme and, as we waited for the mayor to arrive for his official visit, I noticed a mysterious package tucked away in one corner. Now, this was the time of heightened activity by the Irish Republican Army (IRA), and frequent warnings about 'suspect packages'. I felt I had no option but to halt the official party, turn the staff out and then mutter apologies when the bag contained nothing more lethal than a helper's lunch. Thank goodness, I resisted the urge to summon the bomb squad and found out what the package represented by quizzing every staff member in sight.

THE LATER YEARS 🐦

The Aftermath

The impact of GWR150 did not end with the completion of the exhibition train tour. Unsold sales stock had to be dealt with and all outstanding bills and invoices needed to be settled. Then came the final accounting which, happily, showed a healthy profit for the WR and Avon-AngliA.

The last programmed event of this momentous celebration was a lecture on Brunel by Ian Campbell at the Institution of Civil Engineers and preceded by a pleasant meal. Another even more rewarding invitation I received was to a small dinner party for the half dozen or so main trade supporters of GWR150 at which the principal guest and speaker was Harold Macmillan. I found him a very charismatic character and his description of one of the board meetings he had attended as a GWR director was given a very humorous twist when he described the procession of wheelchairs leading to the board room. As a mark of appreciation of our efforts, we guests each received a mounted section of original GWR rail.

A very popular GWR150 sales item had been the sets of postcards featuring former railway posters which the WR had launched using original full-size posters from Richard Tindale's collection. By agreement I took over and expanded this activity, extending the original thirty-two images to seventy and paying a royalty on sales to WR. This activity lasted several years, eventually producing a sales total of 297,000 postcards.

This poster use led in turn to another GWR150 spin-off. Tim Rice of Pavilion Books got in touch with a proposal to use the poster images in a lavish book to be called *Happy Holidays*, with Michael Palin as the writer.

This proved popular enough to warrant reprints and again earned a useful royalty sum for the WR and myself. Just before the work was printed, I had a brainwave that resulted in an agreement to provide AAA with a run-on printing of 500 copies of 40 sheets, giving us a stock of A4 mini posters as a new sales line. Later, Book Club Associates (BCA) got in touch, wanting to have packs of four of these mini posters as a giveaway gift for new members. Packing them in plastic sleeves with a card stiffener was the main hurdle to my response, but a novel solution was found with my wife's help. The youngsters of the William Knowles centre for people with learning difficulties proved both anxious and able to undertake the task and enjoy a reward made up partly of nice cakes! This round of printing, packing and delivery trips to the W.H. Smith warehouse at Swindon followed until over 45,000 mini posters had been sold to BCA, retail outlets and through a partnership with the Jean Pain Gallery in Cambridge.

New Books and Exciting Launches

Books published in 1986 included my *Railways of the Eastern Region (South)* for Patrick Stephens and one with the WR to mark the Severn Tunnel's anniversary, the latter involving quite a few radio broadcast invitations. A new direction was then represented by a call from assistant Eastern Region PRO Stuart Rankin at York, which led to a hurried photographic tour of the Battersby–Whitby line when new Sprinter units began operating there. The result was the publication for the ER of *Cameron's Guide to the Esk Valley Railway*, which was supported by Camerons Brewery. Two more such promotional booklets for the ER were to follow later, one based on the East Suffolk line and the other entitled *Exploring the Tyne Valley by Train*. The latter had its launch in Carlisle Castle, after which Sheila and I spent a pleasant sales-cum-touring week based on Hexham. This new link with British Rail brought me an invitation to PRO Bert Porter's popular Christmas lunch at York, one of those really nice events among very likeable people.

A new postcard line was a double set of sepia postcards of period freight scenes for the British Railways Board public relations people and then a special colour set for the twenty-first anniversary of InterCity in May 1987, celebrated with an exhibition at Bounds Green depot.

I was now to move into a slightly different period of activity, with the book, poster and postcard sales still important but a higher proportion of my time being spent in travel, site and library research for commissioned books.

Both the second ER Field Guide and then a book on the main stations of Britain, both for Patrick Stephens Limited (PSL), involved me in a dozen or so tours of research and photography, taking me all over the country. With three of the existing Field Guides needing updating prior to reprinting, this process was to continue through 1989 with the guide for the northern half of the ER being launched in the York headquarters in the August of that year. Next, the PSL commissioning editor, Darryl Reach, now with the Haynes group which had taken over the PSL business, asked me to drive over to his new offices at Sparkford for a chat. The outcome was a commission to contribute a significant portion of a major work to be called the *Encyclopaedia of the Great Western Railway,* something that was to keep me busy for much of 1990.

Peter Townsend, who had worked for Patrick Stephens Limited and was now running his own publishing company, Silver Link Publishing (SLP), had been a close friend for many years. He agreed to publish a book that I had been thinking about for some time, dealing with the numerous and exciting physical confrontations between some of the early railway companies. Again this involved a great deal of 'field work', Peter accompanying me on a visit to the Saxby area, where a pitched battle had once taken place between the employees of the local landowner and the surveyors of the infant railway company. A short-term investment in Silver Link entitled me to regular and very pleasant visits to the office near Kettering and to our lunchtime semi-business meetings in a pub beside the River Nene.

The book *Great Railway Battles* appeared in due course, but I was already working on the text for a major SLP work on the East Coast main line, including the superb photographs of Brian Morrison. Its launch gave me another very enjoyable outing, this time on the Settle & Carlisle line behind Sir Nigel Gresley. Equally enjoyable, although with no contribution from me, was being invited to Bewdley when SLP's illustrated reprint of Edith Nesbit's classic book *The Railway Children* was graced by a visit from the lovely Jenny Agutter.

Somerset and Railway Tales

In addition to Ian's constant help in all these activities, I had, right at the beginning and with my wife's help, come into contact with a fellow social worker of hers, Roy Gallop. Roy had been a graphics artist and right from the time of my earliest publishing activities had been the main inspiration behind all the book covers. Once I had decided on semi-retirement and had closed down Avon-AngliA and Kingsmead Press, Roy and I began a Somerset adventure that saw us writing Town Trails for the old *Somerset Magazine* and then publishing a series of small booklets on the county under a joint Fiducia Press imprint.

With the physical side of even this local activity taxing my ageing frame, I turned back to my first love with a collection of curious railway happenings which The History Press published under the title *Railway Oddities*. After it came out I received a congratulatory email from an old school fellow whom I had not seen for sixty years. It was Bill Parker, whose railway career had led to the position of divisional manager at King's Cross and who responded readily to my idea of collecting into book form high-interest career stories from former colleagues. Bill's wide circle of contacts proved so fruitful that we submitted and had accepted a surprising three volumes: *Signal Box Coming Up, Sir; Along Different Lines*; and *Real Railway Tales*. Finally, with Ian as my joint author, came another book of railway curiosities which I had given a working title to that effect. However, Amy Rigg, my fine commissioning editor, thought otherwise. It became *The Galloping Sausage*, based on my entry about what the Doncaster Plant staff had called Gresley's highly streamlined experiment, and I had to endure a certain amount of ribbing as a result.

I never cease to marvel at my good fortune in a lifelong involvement in railways and the wider transport activity. It has taught me much, shown me much and led to very rewarding links with some very able and likeable people.

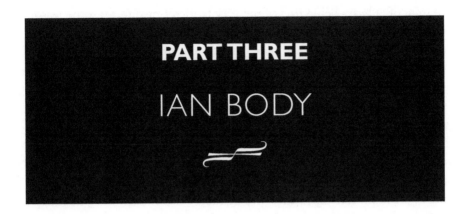

PART THREE

IAN BODY

GETTING STARTED

The Early Days

Railways didn't have a start for me. Being born into a railway family meant that they were just always there. It was where my father and grandfather worked, it was where most of my parents' friends worked and it was the key element to our travel as a family. As a result, it was associated with good things – visits to indulgent grandparents, exciting days out and holidays! With car ownership not being an option but staff-rate travel available (some of which was free), it was the train that gave me the opportunity to travel.

After the period of accompanying my parents everywhere, I moved to travelling on my own with more freedom than those constrained by cost. My first big journey alone was as a 14-year-old from Enfield to Antwerp via the Harwich to Hook of Holland ferry for a few action-packed days spent in the company of an aerial photographer friend. In a previous life he had been Moise Tshombe's personal pilot during the Congo 'troubles' and he retained that swashbuckling approach to life and to his flying. When I went to Sheffield University in 1969, I took my rail travel for granted and, as a result, had considerable freedom to keep in touch with home and to visit friends at other universities.

An Unintentional Career

In spite of railways being part of the very fabric of my life, for some reason it had never crossed my mind to consider them as a career. My first love was economics and so, when the time came to put university behind me and start to be serious about life, I looked only at jobs on offer in banking and industrial production; even being short-listed for the post of mill manager in Peru with Coates Patons. Heaven only knows where my life would have taken me if that had been successful!

In those days there was great activity around the 'milk round', where all the major employers sent teams to universities to conduct initial interviews in the hope that at least some of the long-haired, laid-back undergraduates might prove suitable for further investigation.

It was on one of these 'milk round' days that I was approached by a careers officer asking, in a voice containing more than a hint of embarrassed desperation, if I was free for an hour. On hearing that I was, he explained that he had no one wanting to be interviewed by the railway representative and my willingness to spend an hour in mock enthusiasm for the industry would be appreciated. If only because it promised coffee and biscuits, I agreed and spent an hour being, as I saw it, rather less than enthusiastic about a career on the railways. At the end of the session I was surprised to be told that I was just what they were looking for and that an invitation for a second, and more significant, interview would soon be winging its way to me; not quite what I'd had in mind.

This second interview was residential and spread over two days. As was the fashion at the time, it included a variety of tests and mind games to unsettle the candidates, and I recalled an earlier interview with Lever Brothers involving a member of management sitting on the windowsill throughout the meeting, gazing out of the window. On this occasion, one of the tests comprised fifty questions including instructions such as clucking like a hen and singing the national anthem. Not everyone took the time to read the instruction pointing out that only certain items should be addressed, with a result strongly resembling a scene from Old MacDonald's Farm.

Also included were three interviews. The first was with a manager who pointed out he was a late replacement whose opinion would carry little weight. The second was with a man who was seemingly thrilled to discover that he had known and worked with my grandfather, while the third was equally enthused about the fact that he had worked with my father. Even my natural caution could not deny that this appeared to be something of a 'slam dunk' and the ensuing offer of a job brought about my inexorable slide into railway employment.

So it was that, in September 1972, I joined British Rail as a management trainee in Western Region's West of England Division. This covered a huge swathe of the country from Barnt Green (south of Birmingham) to Swindon and down the south-west of England to Penzance. At this time, the WR was still clinging to its individuality in locomotive power in the form of type-4 diesel hydraulics, largely based at Laira, and the HST 125s were still four years away from introduction. Traditional marshalling yards were restricted in the region to South Wales but serious movement of stone trains was underway from the Mendip quarries and small, local full loads yards remained active at many locations. Bristol Parkway had recently opened to herald a new concept in both 'Park & Ride' stations and serious long-distance commuting, while traditional booking offices were converting to Travel Centres to meet the market's changing needs.

MANAGEMENT TRAINING 🖅

Along with twenty-eight others, I had joined the Management Training programme, an eighteen-month period designed to provide experience in all aspects of railway management and operation with a view to fast-tracking us to our first managerial appointment. Traditionally it covered the necessary area of Rules & Regulations (with exams involved); locally based station, freight and train operation; headquarters support roles; and an understanding of the still significant number of associated businesses such as Freightliners, Sealink, Hotels & Catering and Hoverspeed.

Training Schools

While the bulk of the training was carried out on one's home division, the annual intake came together at regular intervals at various training schools. Of these, pride of place was held by Derby, where the 'serious' subjects were handled. The school itself was run on somewhat military lines with a strict principal, obligatory wearing of ties for dinner and invitations to sit at 'top table'. We returned to Derby on a number of occasions with the emphasis on operational issues common to all parts of the network, and it was here we received our formal tuition in signalling regulations. I must admit, while many took to this like ducks to water, the same could not be said of me. For

A perfect example of the formality of Derby School of Transport in this group photo of the 1972 management trainee intake (Ian is third from the left, back row).

much of the time I wanted to know *why* various instructions were as they were, eventually leading a long-serving and frustrated signalling instructor to provide the revealing explanation, 'Because it's in the book, lad.'

While relatively strict, Derby did have the benefit of being clean and well appointed. The same could not be said of Darlington (visited for public-speaking training), which still quaintly retained dormitories that lent it a rather public school feel, well matched by peeling walls and furniture, where Stephenson's carved signature would not have looked out of place.

At the other end of the scale was the Division's own training school at Westbury, which offered a comfortable, homely and relaxed approach to teaching, with the reassuring operational background reminder of heavy stone trains working through the station to and from Foster Yeoman's quarry at Merehead and Amey Roadstone's at Whatley.

The Far South-West: (1) Signalling
While colleagues elsewhere in the country were plying their trade in southern commuter-land or the industrial heartlands of Lancashire and Yorkshire, I had the luxury of the major part of my training in the more

relaxed atmosphere of Somerset, Devon and Cornwall. Although I had been less than comfortable with the Rules & Regulations classroom learning at Derby, I found myself far more at home in 'real' signal boxes, being able to indulge in genuine hands-on experience. And there was certainly a wide variety of boxes for me to choose from, as the district signalling inspectors guiding my tuition at this stage appeared to have a joint unwritten agenda of getting me to visit every box between Taunton and Penzance, amounting to well over sixty. In this collection was a wealth of architectural styles, signalling systems, staff idiosyncrasies and equipment variation.

Assault

Tiverton Junction had a highly excitable signalman who recorded one incident in the register as 'signalman attacked by fierce gooses birds' after he had been held hostage in his box by half a dozen geese that took a wrong turning and could then not find their way out. This incurred some train delay while he was bravely defending himself.

The vast majority of boxes worked to the Absolute Block system, which ensured only one train could be in each controlled section at any one time. Apart from the larger boxes at Taunton, Exeter, Newton Abbot and Plymouth (which by then had converted to life as a modern Panel Box), the majority of boxes in the South-West controlled little more than a couple of sidings and perhaps a junction; many, such as Hele & Bradninch, remained primarily to break up long sections or because of the existence of a level crossing. It was an ideal way to learn the basics and most of the signalmen were happy to allow me to take over their duties under close supervision. Strangely enough, it was not the operation of points and signals that proved most taxing, but recognition of the various bell signals (many of a purely local nature) and remembering to complete the train register after every operation.

A Bruising

While maintaining safety standards, the staff were not above practical jokes at the expense of trainees. St Budeaux was the junction for the single line to Gunnislake, which itself was already just a stub of the former London & South Western Railway (LSWR) route between Exeter and Plymouth. Here, trains to Plymouth needed to leave the single-line token, which was transferred using a hoop that was caught by the signalman on his arm. In my case the 'second man' handing it over ensured each time that the token-catcher was moving forward at a speed to be added to that of the train itself, ensuring that I would have worthwhile bruises to show for a day's work.

I was fortunate enough to have working time in a good number of boxes, from the large at Exeter West to the small at Stoke Canon. Those with junctions to the main line provided a constant flow of work and variety, such as Cowley Bridge Junction (for Barnstaple), Aller Junction (for Paignton) and Par (for Newquay), while Totnes is a reminder of how times change as I can now have a cup of tea and a cake where once I signalled trains.

The Far South-West: (2) Plymouth

After the grand tour of boxes, it was to Plymouth that I went to start getting my hands dirty, obtaining practical experience of a wide range of activities. My early introduction was on the night turn, dealing with incoming parcels. Every night the main parcels service would bring a full trainload of up to twelve vehicles with the majority loaded with BRUTES, which were independently minded beasts with four stout wheels that refused to co-ordinate with each other. Although we were provided with ramps, the time available did not allow for their use, so we became adept at bouncing the BRUTES to get them off the train and leaning on the back of them to get them to tilt up enough to force new ones into the vehicle. But this was child's play compared to the dreaded Oldham van, which was the only one loose-loaded. This required a member of staff (usually me) to clamber in and rummage around in the dark among over 300 parcels to try to extract those marked for Plymouth before the station dwell time had run out. Our success was measured against the phone call from Penzance to say how many we had missed.

Risk of Showers

From in the train to under the train, I then had a stint in passenger vehicle shunting. My main task was to await the arrival of the Penzance portion of the London services, hop down on the track and uncouple the locomotive. This made its way to the east end of the station, while the new loco dropped back to the Penzance portion with the additional vehicles starting from Plymouth. These were attached together with the electric and brake connections to enable the train staff to carry out their test. The danger, as I found out once to my cost, was that the toilet outlet was effectively above the shunter's shoulder during the coupling operation and not everyone adhered to the instruction not to use the toilet whilst the train was standing in the station.

Other activities involved the platform work of train despatch, freight operations at Friary Yard, introduction to maintenance matters at Laira Depot (with its impressive collection of 'Western' diesel-hydraulics) and a wide range of duties in the relatively new Travel Centre. Here I was introduced to the challenges of ticket issuing, station accounts, passenger luggage in advance, general enquiries and journey planning. In those days there was no computer support for such planning and it had to be done from personal knowledge with the support of the BR All Systems Timetable, a tome of hundreds of pages, different columns for trains that only ran on certain days, seasonal variations, connections that spanned across pages and a substantial collection of codes and footnotes.

All the Fun of the Freight

My next posting was to Severn Tunnel Junction (STJ) on the South Wales side of the Severn Tunnel. Somewhat naively, I thought that Plymouth had given me some experience in shunting, only to be quickly disabused when I discovered the difference between the passenger and freight varieties.

STJ was the largest yard on the Western Region, with over twenty sidings on each side of the South Wales main line. At the time, it came under the control of its own area manager, who also managed the junction station and the traincrew at the small locomotive depot from offices on the Up side. While the yard operated on a twenty-four-hour basis, my turns were all on nights where the activity was constant and hectic and the pressure was considerable. Working on the Up side, trains approaching from the west entered the yard into one of the ten reception sidings. From there they moved on to Undy Hump, where the simple principle was to propel uncoupled wagons up the hump to run freely down the other side into the yard itself. The Control at the summit set the successive points for individual or groups of wagons according to their destinations, leaving the waiting shunters to control the final speed and ensure wagons came to a stand rather than colliding with other vehicles or buffer stops. I was put with an experienced shunter to learn the ropes simply through observation and copying.

Riding the Stick

With the volume of traffic, the constant flow of wagons heading down towards us, the poor lighting, bad underfoot conditions and sometimes poor weather, it was a demanding task, especially for a 'newbie'. Our main job was either to release wagon brakes on the move if the speed was too low or, more urgently, to reduce the speed by inserting a brake stick (like a baseball bat but square in profile) between the wagon brake and underframe, and then to sit on it if necessary to produce the required pressure. 'Riding the brake stick' in this fashion was frowned upon, but the rule was observed more in the breach than in the practice. On reflection, and bearing in mind modern safety requirements, I consider myself fortunate to have survived unscathed but regarded the experience as quite exhilarating.

Operating Variety

With the fundamentals of passenger, freight, signalling and station operation under my belt, the training programme then sought to provide a superficial level of experience of the operating activities.

My locomotive and footplate experience was based at Bristol Bath Road depot, with most of the action being on Class 47 Brush diesel electrics and the diesel-hydraulic 'Western' locomotives which were shortly to begin their withdrawal during the period 1974 to 1979. Most of the journeys were standard passenger trips which could not match the experience of thundering through the pitch-black night between Westbury and Reading at the head of a heavy loaded stone train from one of the Mendip quarries. Never quite sure whether a driver was winding me up or not, I expressed some doubt as to the existence of a toilet behind the low doors in the nose of the Class 37 one night, only to discover he was telling the truth. And when one driver offered me a cup of tea I gratefully accepted, quite unprepared for the fact that many of them drank their tea stone cold.

This part of the scheme also included a visit to the Freightliner depot at Birmingham; a trip across the Channel to Boulogne with Seaspeed (BR's joint venture with the French state-owned rail company, SNCF); and the opportunity to briefly pilot a Sealink cross-channel ferry, effectively controlling the vessel with as little as one finger.

A key part of the overall rail offering was catering and my training included practical experience of waiting at tables on restaurant trains and also, briefly, in the Great Northern Hotel at King's Cross. One of the lessons that catering staff on trains soon discover is to become familiar with the route and track and to know when to brace themselves for noted areas of rough riding.

Divisional HQ Tedium

Inevitably, the fun had to come to an end at some stage and I was directed back to the Divisional HQ in Bristol. At the time, this was split between Transom House in Victoria Street, which dealt with the commercial side of the business, and the Bristol & Exeter Building at Temple Meads, handling the operating matters. These two buildings could not have been more different. Transom House was an uninspiring blank-faced brick and glass building dating from mid-century and containing standard corridors, lino floors and faceless offices. By comparison, the B&E building dated from 1854 when it was built as the headquarters of the Bristol & Exeter Railway. No two rooms were the same, strange staircases and flagstone floors led to unexpected places and there was a 'secret' passageway providing an additional entry to the Control Office.

Although it was difficult, if not impossible, to make this stage interesting, it later proved its value when I moved out to area work. Dedicated staff spent time with me, covering the dark arts of staff rostering, station finance and accounts, and the finer points of standage and demurrage (charges for detention and non-release of wagons). This dedication was probably taken to extremes by the member of staff who wished to explain in detail the focus of his life's work by creating a file designated 'Management and Reduction of Excreta on Tracks'.

Looking back, many of the systems appear positively antiquated, particularly the process of preparing train operating timetables; all produced by hand on sheets with the time across the top and the route down the side, and on which a clear path for a train could be plotted. Similarly outdated was the Control operation, housed in the B&E building and consisting of rows of desks tasked with organising and then managing in real time the activity of passenger rolling stock, locomotives, drivers and guards under the ever-watchful eye of the deputy chief controller, who sat at the front of the room like a headmaster supervising a school exam.

ON TO REAL JOBS 🏴

Seaside Station Master

In an ideal world, the eighteen-month training period is designed to finish with the opportunity to test the trainee out in a genuine job, and our division had traditionally used the position of Station Master, Paignton for this purpose. As a summer-only job it had no permanent occupant, it covered a limited geographical area under the watchful eye of Area Manager, Newton Abbot (taken over by Exeter by the time I arrived), and it had a wide range of operating and commercial responsibilities.

So it was that I headed down to Torbay with my new uniform and my lodgings booked with a cheerful landlady at Kingskerswell to take occupancy of my station master's office, and to take responsibility for the stations at Torre, Torquay and Paignton, the signal boxes at Torre, Torquay and two at Paignton, and the stabling sidings at Goodrington.

The workload very much ramped up during the course of the week. Monday was a day of recovery and paperwork; Tuesday and Wednesday involved visiting all the stations and boxes to keep in touch with the staff; and Thursday was spent preparing for the weekend to come. On Friday the reservation labels would arrive for the Saturday morning trains heading north and during the afternoon and evening these would have to be individually applied above each seat, with every departure usually fully reserved. If all went well, there was time for a brief period of sleep before the heavy boards needed to be put outside Paignton station on Saturday morning. These were used to designate the departures, in order to enable queuing outside the station and prevent overcrowding on the platforms. At the same time, entry to the station was tightly controlled to defeat the repeated attempts by returning holidaymakers to circumvent our carefully planned system.

From 08.30 we would have a departure usually every fifteen minutes, so that by the time the train was moving, the next set of 350–450 passengers would be anxiously forcing their way down the platform. As the train moved out (to be completely filled at Torquay), the next set of empty stock would be coming in from Goodrington and another set of holidaymakers would rush to find their seats. This process was heightened around 12.30 when the first of the longer-distance incoming services started arriving (from Edinburgh, Bradford, Newcastle and Liverpool) for passengers to be detrained and the stock despatched to Goodrington, cleaned, labelled and then brought back for its outward trip. Fortunately, the staff had been managing the same system for many years and had got it down to a fine art, but we were all mightily relieved when evening came and calm returned once more to the station.

Disturbed Sleep at Exeter

When the summer came to a close, Torbay returned to its off-season slow pace and I moved up to Exeter, where I could be more use. I also moved my temporary home to a small bedsit overlooking the Exeter Falcons speedway track, where the noise on race nights made sleep impossible, resulting in a further move, this time to Dawlish, so close to the sea that on wild nights the spray would lash against my windows.

Without a designated position I was free to experience the novelty and variety of this part of the railway. Of interest was the old pumping station at Starcross station, which had served Brunel's ill-fated experiment in atmospheric propulsion for the South Devon Railway. Round from Exeter St David's was Exeter Central at the start of the old LSWR route to Waterloo, with everything clearly exhibiting the difference between the two railways in terms of architecture, signalling systems, colour schemes and station design. Between St David's and Central, trains were required to master the half-mile 1 in 37 gradient which put so much pressure on the Class 33 locomotives that there was rarely enough power to spare for the train lighting, which only came back on once the gradient eased off.

In those days the organisation was still quite formal and the area manager was rarely seen unless you were summoned to his austere office of polished wood, efficiently guarded by his secretary. Although I did not have an official job, my relatively lowly status led me to be the popular choice for the weekly pay run to the various outlying stations and signal boxes, delivering in cash the equivalent of £50,000 in current value together with stores and equipment for every purpose from buckets to detonators.

Back Indoors Again

Once my time in the South-West was over, and having officially finished my management training period, I returned to Bristol HQ for a series of projects until an appropriate formal first posting could be identified. The work was rather an anticlimax after front-line operation, and a month-long task of investigating and recommending improvements for the current system of maintenance and repair to crippled wagons did precious little to boost my enthusiasm.

Having recently got married, I was keen to move from a flat heated only by a paraffin stove to a house of my own. Deciding that Little Stoke (within walking distance of Bristol Parkway) would provide good access to wherever I might go next, I sought the advice of my then divisional manager, Brian Driver, who gave me the assurance it would be fine. I went ahead, duly bought a house and was told a few weeks later that I had been appointed as Assistant Area Manager, Worcester and would have to move home. Another lesson learned.

ASSISTANT AREA MANAGER (TERMINALS), WORCESTER 𝔼

Life in the Country

Worcester represented the last swansong of rural railway management. It covered an area from Ascott-under-Wychwood to Stoke Edith (on the line to Hereford) and north to Droitwich and Stoke Works on the main line south of Bromsgrove, about 60 miles east to west and 10 miles north to south. The management team was fairly typical of the time with an area manager, assistant AM (traincrew and operations), assistant AM (terminals) and administration manager. In keeping with our independence from HQ, we all had our own offices and secretarial support.

To add to the individuality of the office, the area manager had acquired a full set of red leather and rosewood furniture, including his own chaise longue! The local tale behind this is that Lady Foley, who lived on the far side of Ledbury Tunnel, was uncomfortable about travelling through the claustrophobic and smoked-filled tunnel and so furnished her own waiting room at Great Malvern station, travelling there from her home at Stoke Edith by carriage. When she no longer required the facility, it was quietly locked up and forgotten until the area manager decided to 'liberate' the furniture and put it to good use. As a result, he may well have had the best furnished set of offices on the Western Region.

Mixed Blessings

My specific responsibility was for the ten stations, the full loads yard in Worcester, the small freight yard at Evesham, together with its collection of coal merchants, and the area parcels activity. This latter activity was focused on major carryings from the Kay's catalogue company at both Worcester and Droitwich, and our relationship with National Carriers, which handled the standard parcels delivery business from its own depot on the east side of Shrub Hill station. In due course we took this activity over as a direct operation, working from the loading dock on the Down platform at Shrub Hill. While HQ clearly saw financial benefits to transferring the business, it was an operational struggle as we sought to handle the activity in an area less than 10 per cent of that previously available. As some degree of compensation for the challenges we faced, we were well rewarded at Christmas by a major customer who used us to despatch pies, sausages and cold meat. In addition to these responsibilities, there was an on-call commitment every other week, a sharing of the regular visits to the eighteen boxes and manned crossings and the lead role in handling press issues. This was my first involvement with the press, made more challenging as my very first briefing and interview was to explain how we could justify operating trains with no toilets between Worcester and Birmingham; a subject fraught with the danger of misguided humour.

On reflection, life was very comfortable here with complete independence to roam the area, carrying out signal box inspections and lunching in delightful Cotswolds pubs. An additional perk was the opportunity to work most weekends at enhanced pay rates, providing the operational oversight and protection for engineering work.

Signalling Variety

Operationally the area provided tremendous variety, particularly in the number of different signalling systems. Heading out of Worcester Shrub Hill towards Hereford, the line curved left past the junction to the long-closed Vinegar Branch, which ran down to the main road and crossed it at

A typical lever frame seen at Ledbury signal box, which stood at the end of the platform, just before entering the western end of Ledbury tunnel.

135

a point where, unusually, semaphore signals used to control the road traffic. At Foregate Street station, the two lines are completely independent in that, having separated at Henwick, one runs direct to Shrub Hill and the other to Droitwich. Both of these lines were worked by Acceptance Lever between Shrub Hill/Henwick and Tunnel Junction/Henwick. Once the other side of the River Severn and past Henwick box, the system reverted to Absolute Block on its way to the next box at Newlands East.

It was here, on a foggy day, that I arrived to pay a standard visit, during which the signalman received a phone call to say that his wife had been taken to hospital as an emergency. Being of a caring disposition, I told him he could go and I would take over the box operation until relief cover could be found. Only once he had disappeared down the steps did it sink in that, although I had operated many boxes before, this was the first time without some degree of supervision, and this realisation served to temporarily relieve me of any signalling knowledge I had previously possessed. Fortunately, after a word with the signalmen either side I settled into a comfortable routine of receiving and sending trains, together with the operation of the barrier road crossing. But the arrival of the relief signalman was a genuine relief.

Two Tunnels and a Dog

At Malvern Wells box, where the line becomes single, the signalling system changed to Lock and Block; the only example on the Western Region. This modified form of Tokenless Block uses the bell telegraph to communicate between the two boxes and to pass trains through the two narrow tunnels at Colwall and Ledbury, with the line being cleared by passage over a treadle. Ledbury Tunnel was so narrow that doors could not be opened outwards, so regulations existed to ensure only trains with a corridor connection were used to give access to the guard's inward-opening door. In steam days, when a banker was required for the climb through the tunnel, the confined space meant footplate staff would often have to lie on the floor to escape from the suffocating smoke from two engines working flat out. The narrowness of Ledbury and Colwall tunnels led to the installation of an alarm bell wire on the Up side wall, to be broken in the event of emergency.

On the line out towards Oxford, the signalling variety continued with Electric Token working between Norton Junction (where one route diverged south for Gloucester) and Evesham, and then again between Evesham and Moreton-in-Marsh. Evesham saw consternation among waiting passengers one day as the train coming in from Worcester appeared to be driven by an

Alsatian. A driver who had taken his dog to work thought it would be a good joke to crouch on the floor holding the 'dead man's handle' while his pet sat proudly on the seat seeming to be in total control.

Baptism of Fire

The range of operating systems tested me during regular night shifts and weekends in connection with engineering work, but nothing could match the very first week I was on call for the Area. I was a couple of days into the week and less nervous every time the phone rang, so I decided to pay a visit one evening to the locomotive depot. The wind was getting up and I wanted to reassure myself that all was as it should be. By the time I had made my way in, the weather had deteriorated to such a degree that walking was a struggle and various items of unidentified debris were flying around quite dangerously. On arrival, the depot was lit by emergency oil lamps with the electricity having been cut off and, as it was in the days before mobile phones, we were equally in the dark as to the whereabouts of our train services. With all communication gone, we were obliged to use a number of light engines to inspect the line between each pair of signal boxes, to clear whatever debris we found and to collect information from the signalmen en route. Not a single signalling section was without a tree, a garden shed or other blockage which required cutting up on site and disposing of to the side of the track. Although most boxes were still in contact with their neighbours, there was no contact at all with Droitwich box and, as a result, 'time interval working' was put in place between there and Worcester Tunnel Junction. The implementation of this system (under rule 25.a.iv) was so rare that most of the experienced staff on duty had never seen it in action.

With the help of the local civil engineer's staff, things were eventually brought under control to the point where I felt I could go home to my bed. Sadly, the next morning I was called in again as a parcels train, running under the 'time interval' system, had run into the back of a light engine waiting at the signal protecting Worcester Tunnel, with fatal consequences. The whole stormy period had been rather a baptism of fire.

History and Novelty

Like any operational railway, the Worcester area had its fair share of history and novelty. At Worcester Foregate Street station (one of the few remaining high street stations), the original lift was water powered and one of the waiting rooms was suspended from the platform. At Great Malvern the Down platform

Remnants of the past in this photo at Great Malvern showing the covered route to the girls' college and the entrance used for wagons delivering coal for the heating boilers. Buried under the grass in front of the doors was a small wagon turntable.

was joined to the girls' college by a private passage under the road, and direct wagon access was provided from the main line into the college; when I was there I was able to find signs of the small turntable that facilitated the access. At Worcester Shrub Hill there was a 'beer run' under the lines to provide access from the front of the station to the catering rooms on the far side.

In the realms of superstition, a headless horseman apparently roamed the area between Ledbury and Colwall tunnels. More genuine were the notices placed on the drivers' noticeboard advising of activity by the Heythrop Hunt. The hunt believed that this led drivers to reduce speed in those areas and were, on one occasion, observed actually following the hounds into Chipping Campden Tunnel, quite oblivious to the potential dangers and much to the concern of the crossing keeper at Campden Crossing who witnessed the activity. The area management, of course, knew that there was no dispensation for the hunt, but posting the notice did guarantee an annual invitation to the hunt dinner, which was definitely not to be missed.

Freight Tales

A significant part of my responsibilities related to freight operation. Worcester Shrub Hill operated a full loads yard, accepting and creating trains made up from small one- or two-wagon consignments. Early on, my clerical staff tried their luck by rushing into my office proclaiming that there was 'a goose on the yard' and that we had stopped operation. I rose to the bait, announced that I would deal with this errant bird, and headed to the yard to sort matters out. On arrival, I was informed by the yard master that 'goose' was railway telegram code for 'stop accepting until further advised' and that our traffic problems were genuine. Score one to my team.

The yard was a constant source of challenge and mishap. Wagons became derailed quite regularly, but in those days the approach was to deal with everything unofficially and within our own resources to avoid having to complete multiple forms of explanation. Most vehicles were re-railed with little fuss through the judicial use of a wedge, brake sticks and strong backs, and a borrowed Class 08 shunter. More problematic was the day the staff opened the sliding doors of one of the regular Transfesa wagons of oranges from Spain to be met with a tidal wave of oranges, which for reasons unknown had been loaded loose rather than in their normal boxes. The process of reclaiming all the fruit took the rest of the day, even with additional drafted labour.

Away from Worcester the freight activity was limited. Evesham had a small yard largely devoted to coal merchants, who each had their own storage area. One of my unenviable duties was periodically to examine their accounts to ensure they had paid for their coal and to raise necessary charges for the many occasions when they chose to use our wagons for their storage. While I had been suitably trained at HQ for this activity, there had been no indication that the 'accounts' would usually be the multifarious contents of a shoebox. As a result, the business usually resulted in coming to a deal that both I and the merchant were happy with, and in most cases bore no relationship to the actual movement of coal and wagons.

Beyond Evesham the next signal box was Honeybourne Station South (effectively operating as a ground frame), where the junction was only for the daily local freight trip to Long Marston via a reversal at Honeybourne West Loop. Long Marston was home to an MoD depot that rarely had traffic and to Birds Commercial Motors, which ran a major scrap metal operation there. For the MoD it was something of a strategic service provision, while for Birds it was quite a profitable business. It was, however, a costly operation involving three signal boxes for a single return service each day, although the boxes worked limited shifts and had periods of complete closure.

PASSENGER PROMOTIONS MANAGER, BRISTOL 🖝

All too soon my stay at Worcester came to an end, as the powers that be decided it was time for me to move on. Their choice for my next job was in the department of the divisional passenger manager, John Pearce, for which I decided to settle in Weston-super-Mare. The department as a whole dealt with all passenger commercial matters, including fares and pricing, travel agents, special trains, local authority liaison, advertising and working with the various booking offices and Travel Centres. My own task, with my assistant Roy Mealing, was to develop a range of promotions to encourage additional travel and to advertise them suitably. The team was based in Transom House in Bristol, which also housed the divisional manager's office, public relations and those departments looking after finance and the commercial side of the wider freight business.

From a job with total freedom and largely based outside the office, it was something of a culture shock to take up my new desk in an office of around twenty people, where noise levels were high and conversation was a constant distraction.

Competition and Marketing

At this time the railways certainly did not have everything their own way and, from the South-West, we were coming under strong competition from a number of operators. Coach operators were able to attack us through extremely low prices, to which we were forced to respond both to retain our existing business and, equally important, to prevent them becoming the customer's assumed first choice. At the other end of the scale, our business market was coming under pressure from the air service from Newquay to London, which was also managing to make headlines. As a result, our response was split into two with part of the effort introducing and heavily promoting cheap fares, and the other seeking to introduce business users to the services rail could provide and to develop close working relationships. At the time, British Caledonian was trying to publicise its services from Gatwick and joined with us to offer sampling trips to those responsible for company travel arrangements. We developed a very enjoyable programme featuring a train journey to Gatwick and then a British Caledonian flight to the Channel Islands with an overnight stay before returning home, which I personally found difficult to describe as 'work'.

The other string to our marketing bow was the ongoing development of Travel Centres, where our division continued to lead the way. The concept was to convert restrictive and fairly unwelcoming booking offices into a combination of a refreshed ticket office for quick, simple transactions and a travel centre area more akin to that offered by travel agents, in which the customer could discuss travel options in comfort. From the larger centres at Exeter, Bristol and Plymouth, the concept was rolled out to cover smaller stations such as Torquay, St Austell and Penzance.

The 125mph Arrival!

While there was plenty happening in the area of passenger rail travel at this time, the focus was very much on the introduction of the InterCity 125 high-speed trains (HSTs). The first ones ran in May 1975 on the London–Bristol/South Wales route, albeit at conventional speeds of up to 100mph and only on two trips each way, Mondays to Fridays. However, given the significant step forward in design and passenger comfort they immediately caught the public imagination. By October 1976 it was possible to run some of the services at 125mph, and much of the work of my department was focused on exploiting the publicity value of the new trains and preparing the South-West for their arrival, resulting in a constant stream of publicity material, promotional products and sampling trips.

A particular highlight was on 10 April 1979, when we invited guests to join us on the 09.20 service from Paddington to Bristol, to witness what we hoped would be a world railway speed record, although it was not announced publicly. To our relief and everyone's subsequent excitement, the train covered the 94 miles from Paddington to Chippenham in 50 minutes 31 seconds to set a record of 111.6mph and we provided those who travelled with a commemorative plaque.

To exploit the value of the HST service extension we worked hard to achieve maximum awareness among business travellers and the travel trade in Somerset, Devon and Cornwall. Our key activity was a travelling exhibition which we took to Taunton, Torquay, Plymouth and Truro. Not having the budget to hire contractors, we decided to handle the work ourselves. Our Raildrive partner, Godfrey Davis, kindly lent us a small lorry, and we duly loaded up from our Bristol publicity store and set out full of hope and

After introduction on the Western Region, the 125s quickly spread further afield, as in this shot of a Plymouth to Edinburgh service rushing through Bourneville.

good intentions, only to discover our enthusiasm had overloaded the vehicle, collapsing an axle before we were 10 miles out of Bristol. Fortunately, our second attempt with a larger vehicle was more successful and heralded a highly successful promotional tour.

DIVISIONAL PUBLIC RELATIONS OFFICER, BRISTOL

I often found in my railway career that fate took a hand in where I went and what I did. So it was that one weekend saw an incident which produced an immediate vacancy as public relations officer (PRO) for the Division. Not letting the grass grow under my feet, I waylaid Divisional Manager Paul Witter first thing on Monday morning, advising him that he was now without a PRO and that I had brought myself up to speed on current issues and would be happy to step into the breach. Not sensing any particular subterfuge on my part, he agreed and I moved across the first floor of the Bristol & Exeter building to take up my new role.

Good Press, Bad Press

Inevitably, in the way this job had come about it was a priority that I start to create a worthwhile press contact list as soon as possible, and so I made myself widely available for comment and accepted any and all invitations that came my way. It soon became apparent that there were significant differences in the level of trust that I could afford with different members of the press.

An example of the 'good' was with Radio Bristol, where there was a clear understanding of the difference between on and off the record. Key to this was the solid support provided by Roger Bennett, who had the weekday early morning slot where quick judgements often had to be made on breaking overnight news. One particular occasion was on 23 November 1983, when I arrived quite early in the office and immediately put in my courtesy call to Roger to see if he wanted to discuss anything. I was put through to him 'live' and he carefully took over the conversation and stated that he assumed I needed a bit more time before commenting on the Penzance to Paddington sleeper derailment. Given that I had not yet updated myself from our Control Office, he prevented me looking more than a little foolish.

At the other end of the scale was the *Western Daily Press*, where our monitoring of our press releases against the resulting article indicated that a particular reporter was loose with his interpretation. When requests to improve their accuracy failed, I stopped including this particular person on our mailing list until an apology was forthcoming together with a promise of more accurate representation in the future.

Earlier that year – in July – there was an incident which saw the helicopter working between Penzance and the Scilly Isles crash with fatal consequences. We had been running a series of familiarisation trips by rail to Penzance and then by helicopter over to St Mary's in conjunction with the local tourist board. In the wake of the accident and the ensuing rush to produce headlines, one national newspaper stated that safety was so lax that when its reporter had travelled the week before as a guest of British Rail, the passenger list had merely read '1 body' rather than including a name. As it happened the list was under the name of the trip organiser, which was me, and listed my name correctly as 'I Body'! But it was not exactly how I dreamed of making the front pages.

Divisional Demise

Railway divisions had always had a substantial degree of autonomy and this came to the fore when we lent our support to the local MEP, Richard Cotterell, in promoting a new image for the struggling local line to Severn Beach. This was completely rebranded as Avon Metro without a hint of HQ interference or objection and with extensive publicity, but then fell away due a lack of local authority support because the councillors felt they were being railroaded into what would be a costly venture if the word 'Metro' was taken too seriously.

But all good things must come to an end and a major reorganisation meant that the divisional structure was to disappear and all teams and departments would be moving to new offices in Swindon. With one last throw of the independence dice, the divisional manager sanctioned expenditure for a huge divisional staff dinner at the Dragonara Hotel on 21 January 1984. My last project as PRO was to arrange and manage this bittersweet event, which went off without a hitch other than the Control staff working that night wanting compensatory payment!

PR PROMOTIONS MANAGER, WRHQ, SWINDON 📨

The relocation to Swindon took many of the Bristol staff from the stone-flagged floors and quaint, convoluted layout of the nineteenth-century Bristol & Exeter building to a brand new, soulless office block, and from cosy rooms containing no more than a dozen staff to corridors that ran the continuous length of two sides of the building, housing up to eighty staff without a dividing wall in sight. But, that said, everyone was in the same boat and effectively everyone was a new starter. I was part of the Public Relations team which included a PR manager (Ron Drummond), deputy, press desk and a two-person team for promotional work (myself and my assistant, Chris Tagholm). Our job was to put together special events to support station openings, new timetable developments and external partnerships across the Western Region.

150 Glorious Years

Throughout 1985, the focus of our attention was the long-awaited celebration of 150 years of the Great Western Railway, to which the Western Region was the accepted successor. The programme involved a staggering number of events from April to November, with every department looking to play its part.

A major feature was the touring exhibition train, fully described by my father earlier. In addition, the Queen and the Duke of Edinburgh paid a royal visit to Bristol in July to open the Maritime Museum, and things grandly came to a head at the Gala Evening fittingly held in Brunel's atmospheric trainshed at Bristol Temple Meads, evocatively supported by steam-hauled trains in the neighbouring current station.

While these were the highlights, it was the sheer variety of events that impressed. Numerous steam excursions ran; a Region-wide lecture tour was undertaken; Railfreight supported an exhibition of rolling stock and equipment at Newport; and British Rail Engineering Limited (BREL) welcomed visitors to its historic locomotive and wagon works at Swindon. Not to be outdone, even Western Region's Hookagate Rail Welding Depot at Shrewsbury opened its doors for the very first time to the public. My personal involvement was as part of a small group co-ordinating all the events, marketing them individually and as a programme, and providing a point of contact for the outside groups seeking involvement. Given the extent of the programme and the number of partners over the course of eight months, we felt well pleased with the results and considered we had honoured the proud tradition of the Great Western Railway.

New Stations and Novel Promotions

Once GW150 was over we could turn our attention back to publicising current services and facilities and, in particular, a couple of station openings to support the general upsurge of business and revenue.

Tiverton Junction station, the original 1848 junction off the West of England main line, was closed on 11 May 1986 and the following day a new station, Tiverton Parkway, was opened a few miles away on the site of the former Sampford Peverell station. My team organised the opening event along fairly formal lines with David Mitchell MP, the Minister of Transport, doing the honours at the station before a special train took guests to Exeter for lunch and a business presentation. The significance of Tiverton Parkway was its proximity to the M5 and its potential to capture existing long-distance road business through easy access.

We adopted a more public and inclusive approach for the opening of Cwmbran on the Newport–Hereford line the same year, with local schools attending, bands playing throughout and a feast for all in a marquee alongside

Giant figures commissioned at the time of the 150th anniversary of GWR prior to enduring the major effort of 'toddling along' in the Lord Mayor's Show.

the station. This opening was an example of the constant threat to outside events when the heavens opened and threatened to finish it off before it had started. Fortunately, our hard work was rewarded when the sun came out and shone gloriously on the occasion.

In a busy year for promotional events, we were involved in arranging a reception and illustrated lecture in Chepstow to mark the 100th anniversary of the Severn Tunnel. Particularly pleasing was being able to mark the occasion with a limited-edition, special bottling of drinking water under the Severn Tunnel brand.

Not all our work was of a totally serious nature. As part of the general promotional support material for the InterCity offer, we commissioned three 7ft-high models of staff in railway uniform, designed to accommodate a person inside and be able to provide amusing accompaniment to various shows and exhibitions. So confident were we of the quality and novelty of these models that we used them with our entry to the Lord Mayor's Show in November 1985. From personal experience, I can vouch for the fact that they looked far more appealing from the outside than from the inside after several miles of procession.

MARKETING DEVELOPMENT MANAGER, INTERCITY, SWINDON ⟡

A short walk along the corridor of 125 House took me to my next position with responsibility for special promotions, timetable production and marketing, but this time very clearly in support of InterCity. By this time the three business sectors of InterCity, Regional Railways and Network South East had been created to enable a clearer focus and a better fit between the services provided and their markets.

Serious Promotions

While the main national advertising and marketing campaigns were carried out by InterCity HQ, it fell to us at Swindon to develop campaigns of a local nature to increase awareness of facilities and to boost sales. Supporting this was the production of pocket timetables for each of our routes which, with computers still in their infancy, involved a mind-numbing level of detail and lengthy proof-checking. I was fortunate to have two members of my team – Tony Ewers and Steve Claridge – who not only excelled at the attention to detail but also took satisfaction from this work.

Where promotions were concerned, we introduced a special 'Day Out' offer to London and, instead of leaving the production side to HQ, took pleasure in selecting the photoshoot models ourselves and controlling the photoshoot. At the same time, we developed and promoted a range of 'Leisure Pullmans' aimed at the tourist market and offering the same level of catering and quality service as the long-established business versions. These ran from Paddington to Stratford-upon-Avon and Torquay (West Country Pullman), but sadly the public response did not match the quality of service and they were relatively short-lived.

More successful was our approach to the business market, where we developed and expanded a range of Business Travel Offices based in existing Travel Centres and, through a dedicated member of staff, offered companies a complete service covering ticketing, reservations, catering, journey planning and rewards. The concept was successfully spread to other regions.

Fun and Frivolity

Of a less serious nature was our support for Radio 2's operation of an exhibition train. They felt it would help develop their audience reach and we needed to ensure everything went well with what was a quite complex operation. What transpired was a memorable week which impressed a key broadcaster, demonstrated the very best of exhibition train operation and provided us with a fascinating insight into world of radio.

The Monday start was at Reading, where the show was hosted by Ken Bruce: here I have a hazy memory that we managed to tie in a promotion with Persil which involved a girl in a huge washing machine giving away free rail tickets, but where the connection with Radio 2 lay I could not say. Tuesday was a big day, at Weston-super-Mare with Gloria Hunniford hosting a riotous live show starring Georgie Fame and The Wurzels. Wednesday moved on to Plymouth with Jimmy Young, and Thursday saw us at Newquay where David 'Diddy' Hamilton presented the show, incorporating every passing holidaymaker he could find. I did not accompany the train on the Friday, so I am not sure if it went to

Just a few of the many souvenir tickets produced to celebrate anniversaries, openings and sporting associations.

Penzance or St Ives, but I did hear that John Dunn, who was well over 6ft, had some difficulty getting a decent night's rest on the sleeper service the night before.

As part of spreading the InterCity message and image, we were supporting the British Squash Championships. These were held in the atmospheric old trainshed at Bristol, built as the original terminus of the Great Western Railway. The temporary courts were glass on all sides to ensure the audience got their money's worth, and our reward for looking after the InterCity special guests for the evening was the opportunity to play on the same court the next morning before it was dismantled. It was not quite championship level, but as close as I was ever going to get.

INTERCITY ROUTE MANAGER (BRISTOL AND SOUTH WALES), SWINDON 📠

This next move was something of a leap in the dark for me, as it was not something I had been considering and required a breadth of knowledge greater than I possessed at that stage. The InterCity sector (which came into being in 1986) effectively held the purse strings for all activities relating to its services and had the responsibility of (a) planning train services and (b) prioritising and funding the technical and operating services that supported their timetable. Based at Swindon, there were two route managers: one responsible for the London to West of England and Cotswold services, and myself, responsible for the Bristol and South Wales routes.

The tedious part of the job was managing infrastructure cost sharing across the various sectors, down to the detail of dividing the overall cost of running East Usk signal box based on a division of train movements between sectors, routes and engineering departments. The more interesting and challenging part was assessing the value and priority of proposals from civil and signalling engineers for repair, renewal and improvement works, where a high level of technical knowledge was required to make the necessary judgement and clarify the priorities. As a fast-track training course, this job had no equal in my career.

FRANCHISE DEVELOPMENT MANAGER (TERMINALS), SWINDON 🚂

In response to the 1993 Transport Act, the Great Western management established a small, five-person team to design a new organisation able to operate as a privately owned railway, working effectively with the new organisation for infrastructure management (Railtrack) and the rolling stock companies. As such it was a golden opportunity to 'start from scratch' and design a structure as we would want it, rather than as we had inherited it. Early on, Mike Carroll left the team to head up the Region's stations operation and I accepted the offer to replace him within the franchise team, with the role of developing the structure around station management and operation.

It was a slightly surreal experience, feeling cut off from daily rail operation in spite of being based in an office above Swindon station approach. The emphasis was very much on a design that could be justified financially at every stage because we fully expected to be operating it once privatised. It was also possible to start with identifying the needs of external and internal customers and then designing an organisational structure that could effectively deliver.

Much of the end result was down to the personal style and innovation of Richard George, who headed the team and was later to became the managing director of the new company. Most unpredictable were Mondays, when Richard had had the weekend to come up with a raft of new approaches and the day started with a manic whiteboard session, setting the rest of the team off in a completely different direction from that they had been following on the Friday.

BUSINESS GROUP MANAGER (SOUTH WALES), SWANSEA 🚂

By early 1994 the team had finished its work, and each of us looked to where we might go within the newly designed organisation. I was fortunate enough to be given a choice and took the opportunity to follow my heart and return to frontline management as the train services manager for the South Wales route.

In April 1994, I moved home to Cardiff and moved office to Swansea. It had been some while since there had been a senior manager at Swansea and the accommodation was old and weary, but also spacious. Fortunately, a generous budget enabled repair and refurbishment work to be carried out, and after recruiting a completely new management team we were ready to take responsibility for the activity of senior conductors and catering staff on the London–South Wales services and to act as the public face of the London–Swansea operation.

In July 1996, a further internal reorganisation extended my role to include responsibility for all stations and associated operating and commercial staff in South Wales, from Swansea to Newport. This brought the new designation of 'business group manager'.

Flying the Flag in South Wales

The location of the management team at Swansea, rather than Cardiff, was a major boost to the morale of staff, who had long held the view that senior management rarely ventured through the Severn Tunnel and certainly not as far as West Wales. Pride of place in our train service were the two Pullman services: *The Red Dragon*, leaving Swansea at 05.32 for Paddington and returning at 10.00; and *The St David*, running up in the middle of the day and returning as the evening dining service. A full silver service menu was provided on both trains, repeat customers were always recognised and the chief stewards were personally known in the very highest circles. One of the innovations my management team achieved was to reintroduce Welsh beef to the menu against the standardisation expected from HQ.

Being well away from headquarters at Swindon, it fell to me to act as the face of InterCity and much of my time was taken up working with the Railway Users' Consultative Committee and as the railway representative on the Welsh Confederation of British Industry.

A rather different part of the image was addressed when repairs were finally carried out to the upper storeys of the buildings on platforms 3 and 4 at Cardiff Central, which had been badly damaged by fire some years before; at last the station manager had a home.

A New Era and an Old Danger

On 19 December 1995, it was confirmed that the new Great Western franchise had been awarded to GW Holdings Ltd. While there were still a few diehards who turned their faces against privatisation, for the majority it was exciting that it was *their* company that had achieved this first success. On 5 February the following year, the announcement turned to reality and Great Western Trains began to operate on the South Wales main line.

But amidst this overall sense of excitement and optimism, our team was hit by an ever-present reality of railway life. While safety was always in the forefront of every operator's mind, it was always possible that something could go wrong and, on Friday, 19 September 1997, it did. On this day, the 10.32 service operated from Swansea to London Paddington with members of my team as senior conductor and catering crew (first class and buffet). At Southall, 9 miles out of Paddington, the train failed to slow down in sight of two warning signals and subsequently collided with a Class 59 locomotive and freight train of empty hoppers crossing its path. The incident caused 7 deaths and 139 injuries.

Later that day we waited to receive the staff back and everything was done to provide them with time away from work and professional support for the emotional impact of such an accident. For quite a while this incident hung over the South Wales-based teams in support for their colleagues and as a reminder of the inherent challenges of operating heavy services and high speeds.

The Parting of the Ways

In preparation for a major company reorganisation in December 1998, my director approached me to see what I was personally hoping for. He advised me that I would have a job but that, with the relative downgrading of the out-based line management team, I would have to move back to HQ. Having always intended to branch out on my own at some stage, I took this as the opportunity and opted for voluntary redundancy. To give the new team space to bed in before I left, I worked from home from January 1999, liaising over the major Railtrack-funded redevelopment of Cardiff Central and developing a crowd management plan for controlling fans returning to the station after major sporting events.

With the impending opening of the Millennium Stadium and its significantly increased capacity, the Railway Inspectorate had made it quite clear that previous methods of crowd control would not be acceptable. To address this and in conjunction with layout changes at the station, I put together a proposal for controlled destination-based queuing outside the station, with customers being released onto the platforms immediately prior to each train's arrival. This would avoid overcrowding and ensure that customers for later trains would not prevent others accessing earlier services, thus maximising the load for each train and speeding the overall clearance rate. Having finished this work, I handed in the plan which had been approved by Her Majesty's Railway Inspectorate and quietly left the company. Coincidentally, my partner, Margaret, had also opted to leave First Great Western earlier that same year and now we would be able to see if the world really was our oyster.

AVON ANGLIA CROWD MANAGEMENT (CARDIFF) 🏃

Prior to my leaving railway employment after twenty-seven years, my director asked what I intended doing in future. I was rather vague on the subject and hinted that I would probably support my father in further developing the family publishing business. His response was to hint strongly that I might like to take on the implementation and operation of the newly created crowd management plan for Cardiff Central. Knowing absolutely nothing about the practical aspects of running my own company, never having hired staff and with no practical experience of handling large crowds, I sought Margaret's opinion and replied that we would be happy to.

Given that this was May and the new stadium would be open at reduced capacity in August, with the Rugby World Cup (RWC) to follow in October and November, there was no time to lose.

Learning the Ropes

At this point we had a system and nothing else, but fortunately for us, 'Tricky' Edwards appeared. He managed event stewarding company Showsec's operation in Cardiff and took us under his wing. Stewards were organised, contacts were made with barrier providers and we were pointed towards a source of students who were to become the core of our own, directly employed, customer assistance staff. After much worry, work and last-minute panic, we came to the first event on 26 June 1999 when Wales hosted South Africa (and won 29–19). Returning rail travellers were effectively queued outside the station and allowed in just as their service was arriving, and the whole operation went more smoothly than we could have hoped. By the time the final came, with Australia beating France (35–12) in front of a full house of 70,000, we were employing around eighty stewards and twenty

The lull before the storm. Crowd management queues waiting for the post-match arrival of over 20,000 fans returning home by train.

customer assistance staff, and using 300 barriers to move 30,000 people through the station, so we felt we could say we had arrived.

From this initial dramatic learning curve, events built up steadily, with rugby extending into speedway, football, music concerts, rugby league and even cricket. Activity peaked during 2002–07, when Wembley Stadium was closed for rebuilding and Cardiff hosted all the major domestic events for the FA and the Football League. The most challenging time of the year was the May Bank Holiday weekend when the three promotional playoff games were held on successive days, involving enhanced normal services and many special trains. In 2005, the hard work was rewarded when the Football League kindly provided me with a ticket to watch my beloved Sheffield Wednesday beat Doncaster 4–2 for promotion to the Championship, after which I went back to the station to oversee the crowd management operation.

The success of the early events was also rewarded with the request to provide additional control at some outstations (Newport, Bridgend, Neath) to manage incoming passengers. And in due course we also provided security staff to support rail staff on some Valley Lines trains where customers, especially schoolchildren, were particularly unruly.

Incidents, Challenges and Issues

Such crowd control at stations was far from standard in the UK and, to some extent, we were creating a path for others to follow – but it was not without its challenges.

Right at the start, as fans were returning from the RWC final, the lights at the station failed and the emergency generator failed to kick in. Never again will I use a megaphone to joke about not putting a 'shilling in the meter', in view of the hail of coins merrily thrown around in the dark in response. On many occasions we ran out of train capacity on some routes, necessitating calling in road coaches at short notice to take frustrated and angry fans home.

Alcohol, of course, featured in crowd behaviour and greatly troubled the British Transport Police (BTP) when the football events built up. As it turned out, the football fans were relatively little trouble and certainly drank far less than their rugby counterparts. The most easily angered fans, surprisingly, were those attending music concerts, who had a much smaller time window in which to get home and who were far more likely than others to fear being stranded before what was usually a work day.

An ongoing issue for us was the need to clear the crowds onto trains so that public roads and the bus station (which was right in front of the station in the queuing area) could be reopened. As a result, every late-finishing event saw us, in conjunction with our reliable BTP partners, balancing rail safety with our attempts to hand back roads to meet the pressure from the South Wales Police. A key to ensuring that the agencies could work together was the early creation of the Stadium Events Liaison Group, which brought together key transport operators and the stadium management. The success of this group then encouraged the addition of the local authority and event organisers and participants to plan each event in detail and establish clear lines of communication.

Moving On and Winding Down

After seven years of managing the crowds in Cardiff, we decided not to bid when the contract came up for renewal, but to wind down our overall business commitments – although, having done so, we found we missed the action more than we had anticipated. As it happens, our reputation for railway-related crowd management had gone before us and we received offers of work elsewhere, finding ourselves providing our services at Wembley Central, Cheltenham Races, Knebworth and Old Street tube station during major escalator renovation works.

LONDON 2012 – OLYMPIC GAMES 🏴

By 2010, Margaret and I had completely wound down our involvement in crowd management and believed our working involvement with the railways was at an end. Then, in another case of serendipity, I chose to get in touch with Richard George, who had led our franchise development team and had been my boss during my South Wales days. I was only seeking to catch up socially but, with fate taking a hand, a meeting in London for coffee and a chat turned into an offer to join the Olympic Delivery Authority on a six-week temporary basis as a contractor; a temporary basis that started in May 2010 and finished at the end of the Olympic and Paralympic Games, twenty-eight months later.

Olympic Park Transport Integration Centre (OPTIC)

Building on the strength of my work with the Stadium Events Liaison Group in Cardiff, I took on the responsibility of creating a games-time centre at Stratford. This was designed to bring together all the transport operators to share information and ensure the transport activity around the Olympic Park operated smoothly, with well-coordinated responses to any incidents. In spite of varying degrees of enthusiasm from the existing rail and road operators, we gradually put together a facility which became the OPTIC. When complete in August 2012, it had representation from Transport for London, Greater Anglia, Westfield Shopping Centre, the four local authorities around the Park, police and teams managing crowd movement into and out of the Park. My own direct operational team co-ordinating the road activity immediately around the Park were also represented, and comprehensive CCTV coverage supported the whole activity. The whole unit worked in a not dissimilar way to a traditional railway control office, with each section managing its own affairs but reporting to an overall co-ordinating duty manager – such echoes with my past career reassuringly demonstrated that some systems were strong enough to stand the test of time.

Different Cultures

My early career in particular had been very much characterised by a hierarchical management with strict rules and systems being followed and change being gradual at best. Within the Olympic operation, the need to bring all wide-ranging activities together in readiness for a single immovable deadline meant far faster operation and one where the management structures were flat and innovation was enthusiastically encouraged. At the same time, it involved working in conjunction with existing rail operations where the culture was far more traditional and where the priorities were still the normal day-to-day timetable.

The development of effective systems and relationships between the various partners was challenging indeed. The final result was highly charged, highly pressured and immense fun – but only sustainable because there was a point at which it would all come to a glorious end.

AND NOW

Apart from a short four-week period reliving the operational experience of the Olympics at the Glasgow 2014 Commonwealth Games, I have now put the hands-on part of my career aside. My love of railways has, of course, not left me, but now has to be satisfied through travel (with others doing the work) and the joint railway writing ventures I maintain with my father. The railways have been a part of my life throughout and that is unlikely to change now.

By the same authors

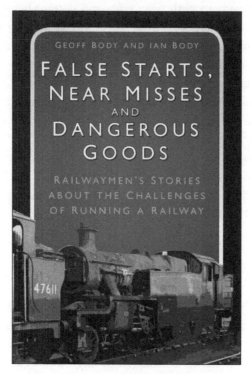

978 0 7509 7027 3

Running a railway is a complex business beset with drama. Fortunately, the highly professional railway staff are ready to deal with these daily obstacles using their expertise, dedication and, as is so often required, a sense of humour. Geoff and Ian Body have collated a selection of anecdotes that illustrate just how unexpected working on the railways can be.

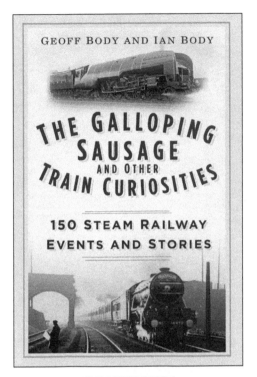

GEOFF BODY AND IAN BODY

THE GALLOPING SAUSAGE
AND OTHER
TRAIN CURIOSITIES

150 STEAM RAILWAY EVENTS AND STORIES

978 0 7509 6593 4

Weird schemes and designs, extravagant behaviour, reckless competition and larger-than-life characters all featured in the genuine struggle of the railway system to evolve. Geoff and Ian Body capture over 150 entertaining snippets, stories, and strange facts from an ample supply of railway curiosities.

You may also enjoy

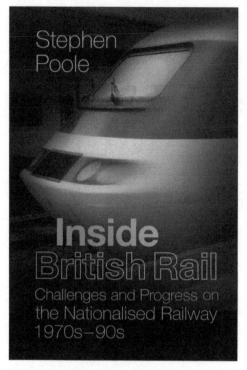

978 0 7509 8556 7

Using his extensive knowledge of the workings of British Rail, Stephen Poole paints a vivid picture of its inner life, set against the backdrop of political, industrial and social change that dominated the last twenty years of the nationalised railway.

The destination for history
www.thehistorypress.co.uk